DISCOVERING

YOUR

SPIRITUAL DNA

Discovering Your Spiritual DNA: *A Complete Guide to Changing Your Thinking and Transforming Your Life*

This manuscript has undergone viable editorial work and proofreading, yet human limitations may have resulted in minor grammatical or syntax-related errors remaining in the finished book. The understanding of the reader is requested in these cases. While precaution has been taken in the preparation of this book, the publisher and author assume no responsibility for errors or omissions, or for damages resulting from the use of the information contained herein.

This book is set in the typeface Athelas designed by Veronika Burian and Jose Scaglione.

Paperback ISBN: 978-1-955546-32-4
Hardcover ISBN: 978-1-0881-2734-6

A Publication of *Tall Pine Books*
119 E Center Street, Suite B4A | Warsaw, Indiana 46580
www.tallpinebooks.com

| 1 23 23 20 16 02 |

Published in the United States of America

DISCOVERING

YOUR

SPIRITUAL DNA

a COMPLETE GUIDE TO CHANGING YOUR
THINKING *and* TRANSFORMING YOUR LIFE

DEBRA A. ELROD

A Comprehensive Bible Study

This Bible study book is dedicated to the Lord, my family, and my church family who were instrumental in bringing it to fruition. It was only made possible by my heavenly Father, Jesus Christ my Savior, and the Holy Spirit. I'm forever grateful to the people who joined my first small group as a beta test for the study and to my husband and daughters who walked closely with me through this process of discovering my own spiritual DNA. I thank God for my new life and pray that my love of God and family, strong faith, willingness to stand for truth, and fear of the Lord will be the legacy I leave to my children and future generations; and that I experience a welcomed reception into eternity.

CONTENTS

CONTENTS

PREFACE

PURPOSE

THIS BIBLE STUDY was created to give believers a simple and practical step-by-step guide to discovering their Spiritual DNA: from understanding how you were designed by the Creator of the universe, to living the life God created you to live, and then passing on to the next generation the key to discovering their spiritual DNA–which surpasses any other inheritance you could give them. By changing the way you think so you align with God's Word, you will fulfill your purpose for which you were born for this generation today!

VISION

That each believer will be:

- more equipped with knowledge and understanding of God's Word and experience the power of the Word in their life. (Hosea 4:6 NIV)

- more aware of the work of the Holy Spirit moving them forward on the path that God designed uniquely for them, to bring out the purpose in them, created before the foundations of the world. (Romans 10:17 KJV; 1 John 2:27 NLT)

- inspired to follow the leading of the Holy Spirit and apply God's Word to every area of their life, everyday. (Matthew 4:4 NIV; Romans 12:2 NIV)

AUTHOR

While I, Debra A. Elrod, penned this study, it was not my plan to ever write a Bible study. This wasn't anywhere on my radar screen. But it was on Jesus' radar! It was His plan, leading me all along and I didn't know it. I'm the author only through surrender to Jesus Christ and the work of the Holy Spirit in my life.

> "Looking unto Jesus, the author and finisher of our faith, who for the joy that was set before Him endured the cross, despising the shame, and has sat down at the right hand of the throne of God." (Hebrews 12:2 KJV)

At 17 years of age, I was planning my future. My plan was that by age 40, I would become a vice president or president for a major corporation. I joined the U.S. Army after high school in part for the college fund. After being honorably discharged, I completed my Bachelor of Science degree in business. Less than two years after college, I started my own business in the automotive industry and grew sales to approximately $1 million annually.

About 7 years after starting my business, I was sitting in the great room of my home looking around, talking to myself. "I've really made it! I should be overjoyed, so why aren't I?" I said. "Maybe when I have a $10 million or $100 million or $1 billion dollar business, then I'll be satisfied!"

I heard a voice say to me, "No, whether you have a $10 million or $1 billion dollar business, you're going to find yourself right back here!" It startled me!

In February of 2005, searching for the answers for living, I decided to read the Bible from beginning to end. I was captivated and started journaling Scriptures.

> "Trust in the Lord with all your heart, do not depend on your own understanding. Seek his will in all you do; and he will direct your paths." (Proverbs 3:5-6 NLT)

> "For the profit of Wisdom is better than silver and her wages are better than gold. Wisdom is more precious than rubies, nothing you desire can compare with her." (Proverbs 3:14-15 (NLT)

After reading this, I said to myself, "Well, I better start getting wisdom." Then I asked God, "What is wisdom?"

Simultaneously, a series of events were transpiring in my business that could catapult sales into the multimillion dollar range. Then I remembered that day in my great room. I said, "Lord, don't let me get to the end of my life having accumulated all this wealth and missing out on what life is really about."

Jesus went to work. In October of 2005, I was listening to a well-known preacher on the radio. She was saying, "I'm talking to someone out there and God wants you, like Moses, to lay your scepter down, so when you pick it back up, you'll have real power!" I began crying and started talking out loud. "Lord, I know You're talking to me, but I don't know how to lay it down. You're going to have to do it for me."

A couple of months later, on December 7, while driving in my car talking to God about a major life decision, I said, "I know the Bible contains every answer for living, and I'm sorry, I've never read it for myself. But I can't cram for this exam! I need You to tell me what to do. I will do whatever You say, because I know You know what's best."

As those words left my tongue, I received a vision and saw myself bowing down with my face down and arm covering my head in the presence of God. I smelled the scent of burning incense coming through my car vents. I looked up into the sky and the sun was moving up and down very quickly, as if it were dancing. I knew what happened to me was out of this world!

It was on this day that I was filled with the Holy Spirit and my journey to discovering my spiritual DNA had just begun!

CHAPTER ONE

MAKE JESUS THE LORD OF YOUR LIFE

HOW DO YOU do that? How does that work? How do I make Jesus the Lord of my life?

It begins with repentance: letting go of worldliness and embracing godliness.

> "If you cling to your life, you will lose it; but if you give it up for me, you will find it." (Matthew 10:39 NLT)

> "For everyone has sinned; we all fall short of God's glorious standard." (Romans 3:23 NLT)

> "For the wages of sin is death, but the free gift of God is eternal life through Christ Jesus our Lord."

(Romans 6:23 NLT)

"Godly sorrow brings repentance that leads to salvation and leaves no regret, but worldly sorrow leads to death." (2 Corinthians 7:10 NIV)

There is a difference between remorse and repentance. As described in 2 Corinthians 7:10 above, remorse is feeling sorry or regretting what you've done, but it brings no inward change. Repentance is an acknowledgement that you were wrong, and you turn away from it and turn toward God to salvation.

The Greek word for "salvation" is soteria (Strong's 4991), and it is defined as rescue or safety (physically or morally); deliver, health, salvation, save, saving; deliverance, preservation, safety, salvation; deliverance from the molestation of enemies.

BEING BORN AGAIN

You must be saved through being born again to enter the Kingdom of God.

You might say, "I was born right the first time," but if that were true you wouldn't need a Savior.

"Jesus answered, 'Most assuredly, I say to you, unless one is born of water and the Spirit, he cannot enter the kingdom of God. That which is born of the flesh is flesh, and that which is born of the Spirit is spirit. Do not marvel that I said to you, "You must be born again."'" (John 3: 5-7 NKJV)

The only way to overcome our innate evil nature is to be born again, to receive the Holy Spirit who awakens our spirit, mind, and soul to the things of God! The Bible tells us that without the Spirit, we cannot receive the things of the Spirit, because they are spiritually discerned.

> "But the natural man does not receive the things of the Spirit of God, for they are foolishness to him; nor can he know them, because they are spiritually discerned." (1 Corinthians 2:14 NKJV)

The sinner's prayer that really changes you comes from a heart change and is linked to true repentance. Below is a sample sinner's prayer. Pray this or something similar as you are led by the Holy Spirit:

> Father God, I believe Jesus Christ is Your Son and You sent Him to die for my sins so I could be made right with You. I confess that I have sinned against You and ask for Your forgiveness. Please forgive me for _____. I also forgive _____, and all who have sinned against me. I surrender and commit to making Jesus the Lord of my life and ask You to send Your Holy Spirit to live inside of me, to change me from the inside out. I ask this in Jesus' name, amen.

HOW DO YOU KNOW YOU'RE BORN AGAIN?

When you are truly born again, you will know it. There will be a distinct change on the inside of you that you will be aware of. You may not remember the exact time or day, but you will remember a time or season when your life was changed forever. When the God of the universe takes up residence inside of you, you will know it!

How do I know? Because it happened to me and countless others I've met along my spiritual journey that have a similar testimony.

The God who put the earth on its axis and the sun in the sky cannot enter a person without them being aware of it. From the point that you are born again, your desire to sin will begin to diminish in your life. You will have a desire for the things of God. You will want to read the Bible like never before. You'll want to know more and more about God, Jesus, and the Holy Spirit. Period! If you have to ask, "How do I know?" then it may be that it has yet to happen in your life.

> "When you came to Christ, you were 'circumcised,' but not by a physical procedure. It was a spiritual procedure—the cutting away of your sinful nature. For you were buried with Christ when you were baptized. And with him you were raised to a new life because you trusted the mighty power of God, who raised Christ from the dead." (Colossians 2:11-12 NLT)

MAKE THE BIBLE YOUR FINAL AUTHORITY

The Word has the power to change your life. However, we can only understand the Word of God in our mind when we can receive it. We can only receive and make sense of the Bible when we have the Holy Spirit in us.

Without the Holy Spirit, it is like reading a history book. The Holy Spirit's presence in our life brings the Word to life—and its transforming power. Otherwise, it is as dead as a doorknob. Reading, mediating on, and applying the Word to your everyday life leads you down the path to discovering your spiritual DNA. The Bible is God's Word to mankind. The Word is Jesus.

The Bible will speak to you as you earnestly desire to receive truth from it for your life. It is alive today as much as when it was written! This is a truth you can depend and rely upon.

> "And the Word was made flesh, and dwelt among us, (and we beheld His glory, the glory as of the only begotten of the Father,) full of grace and truth." (John 1:14 KJV)

> "Then Jesus was led up by the Spirit into the wilderness to be tempted by the devil. And when He had fasted forty days and forty nights, afterward He was hungry. Now when the tempter came to Him, he said, 'If You are the Son of God, command that these stones become bread.' But

He answered and said, 'It is written, "Man shall not live by bread alone, but by every word that proceeds from the mouth of God."'" (Matthew 4:1-4 NKJV)

"All Scripture is given by inspiration of God, and is profitable for doctrine, for reproof, for correction, for instruction in righteousness: That the man of God may be perfect, thoroughly furnished unto all good works." (2 Timothy 3:16-17 KJV)

"For the Word of God is full of living power. It is sharper than the sharpest knife, cutting deep into our innermost thoughts and desires. It exposes us for what we really are." (Hebrews 12:4 NLT)

GET WISDOM

What is wisdom and where does it come from? This is what the Bible says:

"Wisdom is more precious than rubies, nothing you desire can compare with her." (Proverbs 3:14-15 NLT)

"Stop fooling yourselves. If you think you are wise by this world's standards, you will have to become a fool so you can become wise by God's standards. For the wisdom of this world is foolishness to God. As the Scriptures say, 'God catches those

who think they are wise in their own cleverness.'"
(1 Corinthians 3:18-19 NLT)

The fear of the Lord is the beginning of wisdom:

> "Fear of the Lord is the beginning of wisdom. Knowledge of the Holy One results in understanding." (Proverbs 9:10 NLT)

> "The Lord has said to me in the strongest terms: 'Do not think like everyone else does. Do not be afraid that some plan conceived behind closed doors will be the end of you. Do not fear anything except the Lord Almighty. He alone is the Holy One. If you fear him, you need fear nothing else.'" (Isaiah 8:11-13 NLT)

> "Don't be afraid of those who want to kill you. They can only kill your body; they cannot touch your soul. Fear only God, who can destroy both soul and body in hell." (Matthew 10:28 NLT)

When we pick and choose which Scriptures we will adhere to and those we will dismiss, or when we will listen to or ignore the still small voice (the prompting of the Holy Spirit within us), we are lacking in the fear of God.

The fear of the Lord is not a cowering fear, but a fear grounded in awareness of God's greatness, grace, and mercy over us, which will lead us to submit to His will. When we have a fear of the Lord, we will seek Him more in prayer asking, "What would You have me to do? How can I serve You and others today? Where shall I go?"

The fear of the Lord will have you turn away from ungodliness to the one true God of the Bible! The fear of the Lord will push out all other fears, as the Scripture reveals:

> "Such love has no fear because perfect love expels all fear." (1 John 4:18 NLT)

Baptism with Water, the Holy Spirit, and Fire:

> "I baptize with water those who turn from their sins and turn to God. But someone is coming soon who is far greater than I am-so much greater that I am not even worthy to be his slave. He will baptize you with the Holy Spirit and with fire." (Matthew 3:11 NLT)

Pray for the baptism of the Holy Spirit and fire, with the gift of speaking in tongues.

> "John baptized with water, but in just a few days you will be baptized with the Holy Spirit." (Acts 1:5 NLT)

> "Suddenly, there was a sound from heaven like a roaring of a mighty windstorm in the skies above them, and it filled the house where they were meeting. Then, what looked like flames or tongues of fire appeared and settled on each

of them. And everyone was filled with the Holy Spirit and began speaking in other languages, as the Holy Spirit gave them utterance." (Acts 2:2-4 NLT)

The baptism of the Holy Spirit comes from above and gives us power to be witnesses for the gospel in our families, wherever we live, work, and travel.

"But you will receive power when the Holy Spirit comes upon you. And you will be my witnesses, telling people about me everywhere– in Jerusalem, throughout Judea, in Samaria, and to the ends of the earth." (Acts 1:8 NLT)

A PERSONAL RELATIONSHIP WITH JESUS AND THE HOLY SPIRIT

Developing a personal relationship with Jesus through His Word and the Holy Spirit is critical to maturing in your new life as a Christian. Obeying the leading of the Holy Spirit will guide and direct you on your spiritual journey. The Holy Spirit will show you where you need to go, what you need to do, and when you should do it to bring transformation into your life. The Holy Spirit will expose, confront, and deliver you from wrong thought patterns, sinful behavior, and evil influences that have had authority over your life as you surrender your life to the Lordship of Jesus Christ.

"But you have received the Holy Spirit, and he

lives within you, so you don't need anyone to teach you what is true. For the Spirit teaches you all things, and what he teaches is true—it is not a lie. So, continue in what he has taught you and continue to live in Christ." (1 John 2:27 NLT)

HOMEWORK AND DISCUSSION

Share which Scriptures speak most to your heart and explain why. Choose from the ones below or earlier in this chapter:

"But seek ye first the Kingdom of God, and his righteousness; and all these things shall be added unto you." (Matthew 6:33 KJV)

"All Scripture is given by inspiration of God, and is profitable for doctrine, for reproof, for correction, for instruction in righteousness: That the man of God may be perfect, thoroughly furnished unto all good works." (2 Timothy 3:16-17 KJV)

"Trust in the Lord with all your heart, do not depend on your own understanding. Seek his will in all you do, and he will direct your path." (Proverbs 3:5-6 NLT)

SHARE YOUR TESTIMONY

————— CHAPTER TWO —————

UNDERSTANDING YOUR MIND

IT IS IMPORTANT to understand how God designed your mind to operate in the Word.

> "My people are destroyed for lack of knowledge."
> (Hosea 4:6a NIV)

HOW YOUR MIND OPERATES

This section is focused on describing the parts of the mind located in our brain, which has 86 billion neurons. However, neuroscience has uncovered that we have complex, adaptive, and functional neural networks or "minds" in our heart and gut region, and that each of these minds is a sophisticated system of sensory neurons, motor neurons, neurotransmitters, and ganglia. They are able to receive and process information, store it, and access it again when needed. They can sense, learn, remember, communicate, and change.

The heart's nervous system contains around 40,000 neurons called sensory neurites that can operate independently and communicate with the mind in the brain, dubbing it the "little brain in the heart" by neuroscience.

The human gut has been referred to as the "enteric nervous system," or our second brain, and consists of a sophisticated network of 100 million neurons fixed in the walls of our gut. Bacteria in the gut produce neurochemicals like serotonin that the gut utilizes to control basic physiological processes and cognitive functions. Serotonin is a chemical that influences the digestive processes and mood states. Our gut produces over 90% of the chemicals that exist in our bodies. Our gut is versatile in its ability to cooperate with the mind in our brain.

According to recent neuroscience discoveries, memory is a distributive process, which means you can't localize it to a neuron or a group of neurons in the brain, but it is distributed throughout the neural system. This information emerged as a result of organ transplant donors and recipients who could recount information about the donor's life, as well as taking on personality traits they previously did not exhibit.

A pharmacologist explained the strange transplant experiences: "The mind is not just in the brain, but also exists throughout the body." The mind and body communicate with each other through chemicals known as peptides. These peptides are found in the brain as well as in the stomach, in muscles, and in all of our major organs. He believed that memory can be accessed anywhere in the peptide/receptor network.

All this to say, science is catching up with what the Word has been telling us all along! We will discover this as we go through this study.

YOUR MIND AS A COMPUTER

Think of the mind in your brain as a computer. Different parts with various functions working together to produce an outcome. They are hard wired to perform certain functions and to change the performance you need to rewire the system. A serious virus will cause you to begin again.

I learned in my research that there is physiological evidence that when we replace sinful behavior with biblical, godly behavior, new neurons form in our mind and old sin electrons dissipate through our system, giving credence to what Paul writes in 2 Corinthians:

"This means that anyone who belongs to Christ has become a new person. The old life is gone; a new life has begun!" (2 Corinthians 5:17 NLT)

The limbic system is the emotional motor system and is

responsible for the experience and expression of emotion. It is located in the core of the brain and includes primary structures–the thalamus, amygdala, hippocampus–which deal with processing emotions and memories.

- The thalamus can be considered as the hard drive. It is where our gifts and calling are stored. It is also the area of our sin nature. The software designed to occupy this area is the Word of God.

- The hippocampus is what could be considered the RAM. It helps create and file new memories, learning, and emotions. It is also the area where new neuron cells are created.

- The amygdala is the brain's "fear hub," which activates our natural fight-or-flight response to confront or escape a dangerous situation.

Brain structures communicate through chemical impulses passing from one neuron or nerve cell to another. These chemicals include adrenaline, dopamine, serotonin, and norepinephrine.

- Adrenaline: Commonly known as the fight or flight hormone, it is produced by the adrenal glands after receiving a message from the brain that a stressful situation has presented itself. Along with norepinephrine, it is largely responsible for the immediate reactions you feel when stressed: your heart is pounding, your muscles are tense, you're breathing faster, you may start sweating... that's Adrenaline.

- Serotonin: Serotonin helps control many functions, such as mood, appetite, and sleep. Research shows that people with depression often have lower than normal levels of serotonin. Serotonin flows when you feel significant or important. Loneliness and depression are present when serotonin is absent.

- Dopamine: Dopamine is mainly involved in controlling movement and aiding the flow of information to the front of the brain, which is linked to thought and emotion. It is also linked to reward systems in the brain. Dopamine motivates you to take action toward your goals and gives you a surge of reinforcing pleasure when achieving them. Procrastination, self-doubt, and lack of enthusiasm are linked with low levels of dopamine.

- Norepinephrine: A hormone similar to adrenaline also from the brain, which is linked to reactions like arousal, alertness, and attention. When you are stressed, you become more aware, awake, focused. You are just generally more responsive. It also helps to shift blood flow away from areas where it might not be so crucial, like the skin, and toward more essential areas at the time, like the muscles, so you can flee the stressful scene. We have both hormones as a type of backup system.

THREE LEVELS IN THE MIND

In my research, I learned that our mind has three parts and is a vast vault of information stored from our earliest existence in the mother's womb. The three parts of the mind are the conscious, the subconscious, and the unconscious. These were first introduced by Freud.

- *Conscious mind:* The conscious mind is actively processing information. It contains all of the thoughts, memories, sensations, perceptions, feelings, and fantasies which we are aware of at any given moment. This also includes our memory, which is not always part of consciousness but can be retrieved easily and brought to awareness. It is best described when you are in a conversation with someone and are aware of what is being said and can process and communicate relevant and rational responses.

- *Subconscious mind:* A person is alert, but doesn't realize they are thinking or doing something. Your subconscious mind is like a huge memory bank. Its capacity is virtually unlimited. It permanently stores everything that ever happens to you. Its job is to ensure that you respond exactly the way you are programmed. It does not think or reason independently. It merely obeys the commands it received from your conscious mind.

All of your habits of thinking and acting are stored in your subconscious mind. It has memorized all of your comfort zones and it works to keep you in them. It causes you to feel emotionally and physically uncomfortable whenever you attempt to do anything new or different. Even thinking about doing something different will make you feel tense and uneasy. It goes against you changing any of your established patterns and behavior. The enemy knows this and will tempt you into forming bad habits (including habits that look good from a worldly perspective) that, once formed, will be virtually impossible to break. The enemy is well aware of this and can stay hidden, undetected in the seclusion of the mind and soul, or come back another time to tempt when you try to break the habit, do the right thing, or change your mind.

- *Unconscious mind:* The unconscious mind consists of primitive, instinctual desires, memory, and processes of the mind that occur automatically. During our childhood, we acquired innumerable memories and experiences which became unconscious forces (beliefs, patterns, perceptions, subjective reality maps) that drive our behaviors and formed who we are today.

These childhood memories and experiences are memory banks of information that we can't even recall, so it is difficult to access. Your mind manages to remove from consciousness anything experienced as a mortal threat, whether physical, mental, or emotional. It is a part of your being that represses extremely unpleasant memories or hides them away from you, which includes socially unacceptable ideas, wishes, desires, traumatic memories, and painful emotions. As human beings, we are innately programmed by God for survival. This is God's blessing to us to be able to survive in a sinful/fallen world until we are at a place in Christ to be set free, healed, and made whole.

When you suppress an impulse or desire, you're forcing it down below the level of awareness. When you push or repress what feels too endangering to admit into consciousness even farther down, at some point, it's no longer recognizable.

Suppression, repression, and denial are psychological mechanisms of defense. They are instinctual self-protective workings which operate autonomously and drive our behaviors for better or worse. They typically take root in childhood when your mental capacity and judgment are seriously limited. This is also a point of entry for demonic possession, oppression, or demonized strongholds to take root.

Memories and related emotions from dysfunction and trauma in childhood development can get locked into your unconscious mind. Natural defense mechanisms will emerge to keep them tucked away and drive your behavior unknowingly for the rest of your life.

Your defense mechanisms don't grow older as you do. They remain fixed in time and space, all possessing their own will and energy, in order to continue protecting you. They'll relate anything in the present (through chemical impulses) reminiscent of an earlier disturbance as a trigger to make you react as you did, say, at age five. The powerful influence of these unconscious (fleshly), out-of-date defense mechanisms can actually prevent you from ever working through what back then you couldn't possibly integrate and process. Coupled with demonic influences, these defense mechanisms will keep you in a perpetual state of bondage.

For example, consider someone who suffers from anxiety/panic attacks. This can be a result of a traumatic memory locked away in the unconscious mind, and when events align reminiscent of the original trauma, it triggers the exact chemical impulses to react as initially programmed.

> "I don't really understand myself, for I want to do
> what is right, but I don't do it. Instead, I do what I
> hate. But if I know that what I am doing is wrong,
> this shows that I agree that the law is good. So I
> am not the one doing wrong; it is sin living in me
> that does it. And I know that nothing good lives in
> me, that is, in my sinful nature. I want to do what
> is right, but I can't. I want to do what is good, but
> I don't. I don't want to do what is wrong, but I do
> it anyway. But if I do what I don't want to do, I am
> not really the one doing wrong; it is sin living in
> me that does it. I have discovered this principle
> of life—that when I want to do what is right, I

inevitably do what is wrong. I love God's law with all my heart. But there is another power within me that is at war with my mind. This power makes me a slave to the sin that is still within me. Oh, what a miserable person I am! Who will free me from this life that is dominated by sin and death? Thank God! The answer is in Jesus Christ our Lord. So you see how it is: In my mind I really want to obey God's law, but because of my sinful nature I am a slave to sin." (Romans 7:15-25 NLT)

There is a virus in your mind's computer system and it's dictating your behavior. But once you receive the Holy Spirit, He comes in to clean up your system and to empower you to discover your spiritual DNA by enabling you to change your mind and rid yourself of unwanted demonic influences.

As you begin to transform your mind through God's Word, prayer, and obedience to the Holy Spirit's work of sanctification, you can begin to rewire your mind from sinful behavior to godly behavior, as we will discuss throughout this study.

"Then Jesus said, 'Come to me, all you who are weary and carry heavy burdens, and I will give you rest. Take my yoke upon you. Let me teach you, because I am humble and gentle at heart, and you will find rest for your souls. For my yoke

is easy to bear, and the burden I give you is light.'"
(Matthew 11:28-30 NLT)

HOMEWORK AND DISCUSSION SESSION

1. What did you learn that you didn't know before?

2. Neurotransmitters use what to communicate from one part of the brain to another?

3. What are the three parts of the mind?

4. Where and why did God create a part of the mind that hides trauma?

5. Think about a situation where you wondered, "Why did I do that? I knew it was wrong, but I did it anyway." What could have been driving your behavior?

6. Do you believe that when you receive the Holy Spirit, you are free from slavery to sin, even if you're having difficulty overcoming the same sinful behavior?

7. Ask the Holy Spirit to reveal to you what has been hidden in your unconscious mind and what you need to be delivered from.

--------- CHAPTER THREE ---------

SOUL DEVELOPMENT

"You formed my inward parts; You covered me
in my mother's womb. I will praise you for I am
fearfully and wonderfully made. Marvelous are
your works, and that my soul knows very well."
(Psalm 139:13-14 NKJV)

STAGES OF SOUL DEVELOPMENT

IN MY RESEARCH, I learned our developing soul (mind,
will, and emotions) goes through several stages of early
childhood development, which form the foundation of our
beliefs, values, and character that we will carry into adulthood. The messages we receive from our parents, caretak-
ers, and others about who we are–whether verbal, nonverbal, physical, facial, or silent messages–we receive as truth.
Even messages or accusations that we reject have a lasting

impact and penetrate our souls. Any negative inputs can cripple our soul development. This is also where demonic strongholds are waged against the child's developing soul in an effort to keep them in a lifetime of bondage.

Womb to Age 2: This is our true self, a person who has infinite value apart from any other person in the world. During this stage, the child attaches significant meaning to the messages received by parents and caregivers. Bonding and attachment are critical during this stage as they will lay a foundation for the child's future. What are bonding and attachment?

- Bonding is the love and attention the child receives from the parent or primary caregiver.

- Attachment is the child's response to the love and attention given.

- Bonding and attachment together are the emotional connection formed by nonverbal emotional communication between an infant and their parent or primary caregiver known as the attachment bond.

Attachment theory is based on the first relationship that a child has and how that relationship influences the child's mental development. This theory evolved from many researchers, primarily Mary Ainsworth and John Bowlby. It focuses on a mother's or caregiver's ability to be sensitive and responsive to the infant's needs and how that impacts the infant's development. The quality of the bond is critical to a child's future as it will play a significant role later in life in dealing with life's many challenges and relationships.

There are two main types of attachment.

Secure attachment will help develop their thoughts and feelings and build self-esteem. A secure attachment bond that meets a child's need for security, calm, and understanding allows for optimal development of the child's nervous system. A child's developing brain organizes itself to provide a foundation based on a feeling of safety. As a child matures, this foundation can result in healthy self-awareness, eagerness to learn, empathy, and trust.

Insecure attachment will have an opposite effect of secure attachment with deep insecurities. They are often caused by misattuned parenting, childhood trauma, or abuse. If you have an insecure attachment style, you avoid closeness with others and your whole existence depends on it.

Age 2 to 6: Our true self is modified by what our parents or caregivers allow or don't allow. Bonding and attachment continue. This is the stage of imagined power. During this stage, the child is able to attach significant meaning to the messages of others, whether verbal or nonverbal. The more the imagination is allowed to flourish, the greater the range of choices for later in life.

Age 6 to 12: The self is altered. This is the stage of pretend power and freedom. Comments made as to the character, worth, and abilities of the child are internalized. When parents or primary caregivers are very forceful or effective in what is said about the child, the impression is more difficult to remove, as if the information becomes encapsulated or "wired" into the developing soul (mind), forever protected (unconscious mind), and able to become more influential as time passes.

Age 13 to 19: This is the trial self. During this stage, the adolescent may believe or reject messages received thus far, but is not certain either way. He/she must gather the strength to experiment with various trial personalities to find the one that is suitable for the peer group they think they should belong to.

The most important emotional needs for every human being throughout their life are affirmation of the true self and unconditional love. The most valuable gift you can give your child is love.

During each stage of soul development, it is critical that the child's most basic emotional needs of affirmation of the true self and unconditional love be met, as unmet emotional needs will be an open door for deception from the flesh, the world, and the enemy.

However, even the most loving and committed parents cannot always meet the child's needs and communicate the truth about the child to the child at all times. The only source for the truth about an identity is God as written in the Word of God. The greatest love that any of us receive is *agape* love (true unconditional love), which only comes from God the Father through Jesus Christ and the Holy Spirit.

HOMEWORK AND DISCUSSION SESSION

1.   When does the soul development process begin?

2.   Which stage of soul development is the most critical?

3.   What is the attachment bond?

4.   What are the most important human emotional needs?

5.   Who is the only source for the truth about a person's identity?

Take time to reflect and share what you have learned and any experiences as the Holy Spirit leads.

CHAPTER FOUR

SOUL DYSFUNCTION

THERE ARE SEVERAL dysfunctions that might result from trauma during soul development.

Early childhood soul development lays the foundation for our beliefs, values, and character as we progress through life, introduced in the previous chapter. What steel is for the foundation of a building, early childhood soul development is for the foundation of our life. Scripture reveals that any foundation that is not built upon the rock when the rains and floods come will collapse with a mighty crash.

> "When the rains and floods come and the winds beat against that house, it will collapse with a mighty crash." (Matthew 7:27 NLT)

EFFECTS OF TRAUMA

Could the origin in which nervous breakdowns and other mental illnesses occur be traced back to trauma experienced in the early childhood stages of soul development? Let's explore the effects of trauma on the developing soul.

Womb to Age 2: Our True Self

We learned that bonding and attachment form the attachment bond of either a secure or insecure attachment. When trauma and dysfunction play a role in the attachment bonding, an insecure attachment bond will most likely develop.

What can result from an insecure attachment bond?

An insecure attachment bond is one that does not meet a child's need for security, calm, and understanding. It can hinder a child's brain development for optimal organization. It can also restrain mental, emotional, and physical development, which can result in learning problems and difficulty in forming relationships as the child matures.

Infants who are insecurely attached do not trust easily, having learned that adults are not reliable. They tend to avoid others; refuse interaction with others; show anxiety, anger, or fear; and exaggerate distress, which falls into an anxious, avoidant, or disorganized insecure attachment style.

Age 2 to 6: Our True Self is Modified

As we learned, this is the stage where imagination plays a significant role in the child's development.

During this imaginary stage, if a child experiences trauma which interrupts their emotional development, they can get stuck in this age bracket emotionally while still growing physically. Their reasoning process will lean toward fantasy thinking in areas where the emotions are involved, primarily relational, well into their adulthood.

For example, girls will be looking for their knight in shining armor to marry who will protect and save them, while boys will be driven to be the rescuer and savior. These will result in a futile attempt, regardless of the vigor on the part of the either mate, for until the original need is met, it will remain open. The enemy of our soul does not play fair and a primary target for demonic oppression and establishing long-term strongholds is in the mind of a child. The enemy will use temptation and deception to lure a child's mind into behaviors to meet their own needs, before they can make a decision to turn toward God.

Age 6 to 12: The Self is Altered

This is the stage where the child internalizes everything they receive about themselves and it is embedded in the mind of the developing soul, becoming more protected as time goes on. When severe trauma of abuse is experienced, the child can grow to disdain human beings to the point of loathing, hating, plotting their revenge, and/or wanting their abuser punished. This can be so concealed in the unconscious mind that when triggered and demonically influenced, a person who seemingly lived a normal life can exhibit violent outbursts or become a kidnapper or a murderer, much to the surprise of their neighbors and friends and even the family where the abuse was perpetuated.

Age 13 to 19: The Trial Self

This is the stage where the child should be experimenting with trial personalities that they find fit them and their friend group. However, trauma experienced during the previous developmental stages will impede their progression to attempt or fully engage in this stage. The more serious the trauma they experienced, the more likely the personality they take on will be far removed from their true self, which at this point is securely hidden from exposure. Rebellion, drugs and alcohol, and various other defeating mentalities and behaviors are the resulting symptoms of a dysfunctional soul.

PSYCHOLOGICAL BEHAVIOR DYSFUNCTIONS

Trauma experienced during early childhood soul development can produce numerous psychological behavioral dysfunctions. We will focus on three widely acknowledged psychological dysfunctional behaviors and the connection with demonic infiltration of the soul. These are trauma bond, arrested development/fixation, and pseudo personality/false self.

Trauma Bond

Trauma Bond is a psychological response to abuse. It is created when an abuser uses mental, physical, and/or emotional abuse and the abused person forms an unhealthy bond with the person that abuses them. The trauma bond becomes reinforced through cycles of abuse followed by remorse, which ultimately keeps the victim from escaping the relationship.

In early childhood, behaviors that appear to be signs of attachment are actually seriously confused interactions which reverse the purpose of a healthy attachment and have as their purpose the protection of the abuser by the child. These displays of loyalty are bred upon fear and survival concerns on the part of the child.

A child trapped in an abusive environment must find a way to adapt. They must find a way to preserve a sense of trust in people who are untrustworthy, safety in an unsafe environment, control in a terrifying unpredictable situation, and power in a state of helplessness. Unable to care and protect themselves, they must make up for the failures of adult care and protection with an immature psychological defense system.

So they form this trauma bond because they rely on the abusive parent or caregiver to fulfill emotional needs of love and support. They will then associate love with abuse. The child will also blame themselves for the abuse as a way of making sense of what is happening to them. This allows the caregiver to continue being "good" in the child's eyes, which reinforces the bond.

The unhealthy trauma bond also becomes reinforced neurologically by the release of mind chemicals (endogenous opioids) which alleviate stress and pain and enhance mood, which may then intensify the bond. The child's loyalty to the abuser becomes stronger as they view their survival in the hands of an abusive parent or caregiver. The process of survival, pleasing the parent, and constantly adapting to a harsh and unsafe environment will rob the child of their childhood.

Unbeknownst to the child, these behaviors will be a part of their psychological makeup that they will carry into adulthood. They will naturally be attracted to other relationships (friendships/mates) that continue the established chemical releases in their brain of the trauma bond. This bond is played out in the life of a married couple where the wife continues to go back to an abusive husband and professes, "He didn't mean it. He really loves me!" She is helpless to break free from a flesh/neurological perspective and supernaturally from demonic influences ensuring the bond remains.

Arrested Development or Fixation

In my research, I learned that traumatic events during childhood activate the adrenaline chemical and push away the other chemicals (dopamine, serotonin, and norepinephrine) needed to reach the age of decision, which is between 9 and 13 years of age.

Trauma during childhood development causes an interruption or a halt in your soul's emotional development. While you continue to grow outwardly, your emotional development is locked up and you act out when stressed. It manifests itself especially in relationships. It will surface during what is a perceived "stressful" situation from the defense mechanisms stored in your unconscious mind.

You can be forty years old, but when triggered, you react like a five year old. A female will have fantasy thinking about her mate and relationship, whereas a male will control sex and money. This is referred to as "arrested development" in Christian counseling ministries and "fixation" in mental health communities.

There are several types of traumatic events that can arrest emotional development in early childhood: rejection; verbal, emotional, and physical abuse; abandonment; neglect; and sexual abuse, incest, and molestation, which can occur from the womb through adolescence (which is the most critical phase of human emotional development).

Rejection is the worst form of the abuses; however, each is a form of rejection, as discussed below.

- *Rejection*: This is one of the most severe forms of abuse, as it withholds love, which is a critical component for each human being's existence. An absence of love is as damaging to the person's soul as death is to the body. It is also a weapon in the hands of the enemy of our soul to disturb, distort, and disintegrate the development of the personality, leading to schizophrenia as detailed by Ida Mae Hammond's revelation during deliverance ministry. I also learned in my research that the enemy will attempt to project his own rejection upon us to make us doubt our redemption, because he is rejected once and for all with no way for redemption.

  Rejection comes in many shapes and sizes: a child experiencing isolation from one parent or the other through divorce, overhearing a parent share they didn't plan to have a baby and really didn't want one, the child was a mistake, or giving up a child for adoption. Favoritism among siblings by the parent(s) or anything the child perceives as withholding love, including sending your child off to preschool too early, where the child believes in their mind that they are being rejected by their mother/caregiver. This and other forms of rejection develop a lack of self-worth and are debilitating to the child's soul development.

- *Verbal abuse*: Constant criticism, put-downs, and rejection; demeaning and derogatory comments about your looks, behavior, or actions; cursing; and name calling are all forms of verbal abuse. Other not-so-noticeable abuse includes comments such as, "You're too sensitive. You can't take a joke." It defines your inner world. The abuser attempts to say they know what you are thinking or doing. A baby is crying in the middle of the night and the parent or caregiver screams, "Shut up, stop crying, and go to sleep. We don't want to hear it anymore!" These forms of verbal abuse create wounds in the child's developing soul–or adult's developed soul–and will hinder our walk with the Lord until they are healed.

- *Physical abuse*: Physical abuse can look like taking a blow to the head; being thrown across a room or against a wall or object; or getting slapped, whipped, or punched in any area of the head or body. When a child experiences this kind of abuse in early childhood, they view trusting as life-threatening and conclude that this abusive parent wants them dead, which they perceive that it must be they don't deserve to live. This opens the door to demonic possession, oppression, and demonization from spirits of death, hate, anger, rage, bitterness, and others.

- *Emotional abuse*: Emotional abuse is a pattern of behavior that creates fear and centers around control, manipulation, isolation, and demeaning or threatening behavior by using emotions to criticize, embarrass, shame, blame, or otherwise manipulate a person. In general, a relationship is emotionally abusive where there is a consistent pattern of abusive words and bullying behaviors that wear down a person's self-esteem and undermine their mental health, causing them to doubt their perceptions and reality. A parent or caregiver can use emotionally manipulative tactics after abusive actions to appeal to the child's need for security and love by telling the child how sorry they are; showering them with gifts, attention, and affection; or making a secrecy oath to never let it happen again, only to have the abusive behavior repeated. It is a Dr. Jekyll/ Mr. Hyde environment or what is considered "double mindedness."

- *Emotional parentification abuse*: This happens when a child becomes the parent's counselor, confidant, or emotional caretaker, and it usually occurs when parents are unhappy in their own marriage or dissatisfied with their lives. They might tell the child about their frustrations, cry excessively, complain about their relationships, or even hurt themselves in front of the child. Whatever it is that they share with the child, it is too much for their young psyche to handle.

Every child who senses or is made aware of their parent's unhappiness, fear, or other distress will try to "fix" it. They will take it upon themselves as their own personal responsibility, often for life, to fix their parent. Their attempts to rescue their parent will undoubtedly fail and they'll believe it's their fault. They'll get caught in a bondage of the impossible, which is a root of depression and an open door for the demonic realm.

- *Parentification*: This can be viewed as a role reversal of the child and parent. Children take on the task of rescuing mother and/or father in an effort to make them happy so, in return, the parents can meet the child's needs. However, it is destined for failure as no one has this ability; however, in the child's mind, it's their fault. A child takes on 100% responsibility for everything that goes wrong during their upbringing.

A child can also have a role assignment even before conception and birth. For example, when a woman becomes pregnant in order to get a man to marry her or to save a marriage or any other means the parents deem necessary. Thus, the role reversal of child/parent in an effort on the part of the child to solve the parent's problems is at play. No matter what age in the development process, trying to solve someone else's problems is a prescription for failure and is a major root of depression in adolescence or early adulthood.

The effects of parentification are long-lasting in cases of extreme abuse and violence found in unpredictable households of drug, alcohol, or other addictions. As research indicates, women tend to seek their fathers in their husbands knowingly or unknowingly. Daughters will undoubtedly seek out and marry mates that mirror their father in an attempt to have their unmet needs met in the body of another man who is now available–or so they think. This inevitably turns into a love/hate relationship: on one hand, she being overly jealous and protective, and on the other, she has a desire to reject and punish her mate as a vent of internal emotional rage. However, this is all displaced when her mate begins to indulge in the same addictions of her father and she regresses to her childhood mental programming and the cycle continues.

Any child caught up in a bond of trying harder in an attempt to change their parents by being peacemakers or trying to protect one parent from the other during their developmental years will undoubtedly take on the label of failure and will spend the rest of their life trying to prove otherwise. They will tend to become overachievers, people pleasing, and prone to relationships that resemble the ones from their childhood, usually with unreasonable, demanding, inconsistent, and even tyrannical people.

Pseudo Personality/False Self

A false self is created during our soul development to ward off mounting anxiety to keep the true self safe and often hidden or to help a family to maintain its denial of problems.

It is an adaptive (maladaptive) reaction to a dysfunctional

situation. When a child is abused by a person they count on the most during the trust versus mistrust stage (infancy–elementary school age), the message about self is that trusting is life-threatening. The abuse causes a child to internalize deep within their being that there is something wrong with them, and both power and sense of becoming are suspended or removed.

Exploration of the true self is halted and the pseudo personality/false self begins to take over. This false self functioning becomes compulsive and unconscious to the person wearing this mask. However, the enemies of our soul (the devil and his demonic forces) know all too well our natural blood line and sin nature. These demonic forces are assigned to us to ensure we maintain the false self at all costs. This is an open door for demonic oppression.

This false self becomes our "ideal self," because our true self (usually in childhood) felt too weak, inadequate, or overwhelmed to function and gain approval. We constructed a version of self that was better, stronger, and more able to cope well, a self that was less easily wounded, made anxious, or devastated. For example, bullying becomes "strength" and manipulation or controlling becomes cleverness or even compassion.

A false self is an unconscious defense mechanism, which can stifle the growth of a conscious, authentic self. It's the false self that strategizes and develops strength, confidence, and acceptance. To convince everyone around us how good/mature we are, we take on a pseudo personality that fits with the people we're around. Because it is buried deep into our unconscious mind, the person with the false self would never know that it's false, and if you were to challenge them on it, they would see you as the problem, not themselves, and they would probably begin analyzing your need to criticize.

The false self is there to hide, ward off, or cope with unfelt, unacknowledged pain, and when you challenge the behavior–whether it be compulsive lying, talking, joking, chronic cuteness, or intellectual superiority–you challenge the pain. The hurt that is hiding gets somehow triggered or touched, and anger or retaliation, fleeing or removing themselves may result. It is a coping strategy. It is a mental stronghold which embodies a double minded personality that is fueled by demonic possession, oppression, and/or demonization. This is also known as schizophrenia in the mental health community and described in detail in the deliverance ministry of Ida Mae Hammond's schizophrenia revelation.

"A double minded man is unstable in all his ways." (James 1:8 KJV)

HOMEWORK AND DISCUSSION SESSION

1. What foundation is laid during early childhood soul development?

2. What can be a result of an insecure attachment bond?

3. What are the three widely known psychological dysfunctional behaviors discussed?

4. What psychological dysfunctional behavior stands out the most to you? Why?

5. Why is a false self developed and what fuels it?

Take time to reflect and share what you have learned and any experiences as the Holy Spirit leads.

---------- CHAPTER FIVE ----------

SOUL CURE AND DELIVERANCE

G OD, IN HIS goodness to mankind and loving us in
our humanness, provides healing in the form of med-
icines and medical procedures for illnesses, diseases, and
broken limbs of all kinds, including the mind, through the
medical community and psychiatry.

I'm not a licensed psychiatrist or medical professional.
My background and degree are in business with a Bach-
elor of Science in business administration and honorably
discharged from the U.S. Army as a medical specialist.
However, the Lord brought me into the Kingdom of light.
Through the gospel of Jesus Christ, the leading of the Holy
Spirit, and a gift of knowledge, I was led to research how

we develop psychologically and these are my assertions, so please confirm them for yourself.

As I was researching and reading the various behavioral models, it became apparent in my understanding that there were numerous things that could go wrong at any point throughout our psychological developmental process, as discussed in the previous chapters. The only "physician" that knows exactly where you need healing and deliverance is Jesus Christ, through the power of the Holy Spirit, and in the name of Jesus! I pray that as you continue reading, the Holy Spirit will enlighten your heart and mind to receive what you need specifically for your complete healing and deliverance.

SECULAR CURE FOR SOUL DYSFUNCTIONS

The secular mental health community prescribes medicine to regulate a person's brain chemicals. They also provide counseling to aid the person in sharing information about themselves that result in causing them the most stress and attempt to gather information from the recesses of the person's mind which may be the contributing factor causing their issues and, once released, can alleviate their pain and symptoms.

These methods can be effective when utilized. However, the secular health community has no prescription to restart the mind's maturation process, as they believe once the brain is fixed, it cannot be restarted; hence, they refer to this condition as fixation. Nor can they reach to the inside core of the person's issues, because it is unseen and unknown and can have generational spiritual origins.

CHRISTIAN CURE FOR SOUL DYSFUNCTIONS

The Christian community prescribes the preaching, teaching, and *rhema* Word toward repentance, forgiveness, and transformation; inner healing, sanctification, and deliverance from demonic oppression, and demonization through casting out demons, which can only be done in the name of Jesus and the power of the Holy Spirit.

> "At that very time, Jesus cured many people of their diseases, illnesses, and evil spirits, and he restored sight to many who were blind." (Luke 7:21 NLT)

In my research and experience, I learned the brain can be restarted through the process of transforming a person's mind with the Word of God, by drinking in the Word into one's soul like drinking in medicine, along with adherence and obedience to following the leading of the Holy Spirit and applying the Word.

The Word and the Holy Spirit have the power to take an ax to the root to rewire the mind around trauma, produce new neurons, release the proper chemicals, heal our wounds, develop our personality to be more like Jesus, and deliver us from demonic infiltration.

"For what is impossible with man is possible with God! For with God nothing will be impossible." (Luke 1:37 NKJV)

"For the weapons of our warfare are not physical (weapons of the flesh and blood), but they are mighty before God for the overthrow and destruction of strongholds, (inasmuch as we) refute arguments and theories and reasonings and every proud and lofty thing that sets itself against the (true) knowledge of God, and we lead every thought and purpose away captive into the obedience of Christ (the Messiah, the Anointed One)." (2 Corinthians 10:4-5 AMPC)

It is impossible for any person regardless of their intellect or education, saved or unsaved, to know exactly where a person needs inner healing and deliverance apart from the one true God—Father, Son, and Holy Spirit—who formed that person in their mother's womb. Thus, the only place for complete healing and wholeness is the doctor's office of Jesus Christ and the work of the Holy Spirit.

DELIVERANCE FROM A DYSFUNCTIONAL SOUL AND DEMONIC INFILTRATION

So how does one seek deliverance from a dysfunctional soul or demonic infiltration?

1.   1. *Ask the Holy Spirit to reveal the truth to you.* Be will-

ing to face the truth of sin, lies, and/or trauma that has held you captive. As difficult or painful as the process may be, repent of any convicted sin, come out of agreement with lies you've believed, and let go of any trauma from your past that has defined you as a person.

2. *Discover who you are in Christ.* Ask God to show you your true self. God created you to be a person of infinite value, who is loved beyond measure apart from any other person in the world! You are someone Jesus came to die for, and He shed His blood so you could be made right in the sight of God and spend eternity with Him. This is discussed further in chapter 7.

> "Even if my mother and father abandon me, the Lord will hold me close." (Psalm 27:10 NLT)

> "For we are His workmanship, created in Christ Jesus for good works, which God prepared beforehand that we should walk in them." (Ephesians 2:10 NKJV)

3. *Release anger and forgiveness.* If you are aware that anger lies underneath your actions, it has to be discharged. Rage and anger are pain in the true self. In order to discharge the anger, it must be directly aimed at the offender by letting them know what they did was wrong and hurtful and to never do it again. There are several ways this can be accomplished, either by going directly to the offender, writing a letter to them, or if the per-

son has passed, having an open conversation as if they were present sitting across a table from you. The key is to have no expectations on how they will respond. It doesn't matter one way or the other; it's for you to be set free from the anger. Then forgive the offender and ask the Holy Spirit to help you to forgive, if you're having difficulties, and to guide you through forgiveness. This is in line with the first part of correcting a fellow believer.

"If another believer sins against you, go privately and point out the fault." (Matthew 18:15a NLT)

Even if the person is a non-believer, your father or mother, natural brother or sister, or friend, God's method still works to cleanse the believer from the trauma and emotional conflict they have experienced.

4. *Drop the false self and start again.* You have to come out of agreement with all false selves and renounce any and all involvement in the demonic realm and generational sin that received its power from misinformation and impossibilities. Declare them all lies! You have to permanently drop the false self and start again in light of the facts from the Word of God! Yes, we are born with a sin nature, but we are not rejected. We have redemption through the shed blood of Jesus Christ to be accepted by the Father and to live out our God-given destiny.

"Throw off your old sinful nature and former way of life which is corrupted by lust and deception. Instead, let the Spirit renew your thoughts and attitudes. Put on your new nature, created to be like God–truly righteous and holy." (Ephesians 4:22-24 NLT)

5. *Stop blaming.* Stop blaming your own bad/wrong behavior on what happened or what someone else did to you or didn't do for you. Confess and break agreement with all ungodly soul ties in your past and generationally. Any trauma you experienced should not be used as an excuse for not working on changing your own behavior. Continuing to place the blame on a circumstance or person makes it easier for our flesh to stay in its subconscious comfort zone and be demonically enticed. We have to "own" our own behavior and be willing to stop it in order to change it. We have to grow up and change, as the Scripture says.

"When I was a child, I spoke as a child, I understood as a child, I thought as a child; but when I became a man (woman), I put away childish things." (1 Corinthians 13:11 NKJV)

"Do not let sin control the way you live; do not give in to sinful desires. Do not let any part of your body become an instrument of evil to serve sin. Instead, give yourselves completely to God, for you were dead, but now you have new life. So, use your whole body as an instrument to do what is right for the glory of God." (Romans 6:12-13 NLT)

6. *Break old habit patterns.* Whether it is a corrupt flesh or demonic oppression or demonization, you must be willing to break old habit patterns, which your flesh will battle against. You must resist evil thoughts and desires and come out of alignment with demonic spiritual forces who may work fervently to stay undetected, but will show themselves unexpectedly in your own behavior.

"Can two people walk together without agreeing on the direction?" (Amos 3:3 NLT)

"So put to death the sinful, earthly things lurking within you. Have nothing to do with sexual sin, impurity, lust, and shameful desires. Don't be greedy for the good things of this life, for that is idolatry." (Colossians 3:5 NLT)

"But now is the time to get rid of anger, rage, malicious behavior, slander, and dirty language. Don't lie to each other, for you have stripped off your old evil nature and all its wicked deeds. In its place you have clothed yourselves with a brand-new nature that is continually being renewed as you learn more and more about Christ, who created this new nature in you." (Colossians 3:8-10 NLT)

"Since God chose you to be the holy people whom He loves, you must clothe yourselves with tenderhearted mercy, kindness, humility, gentleness, and patience. You must make allowance for each other's faults and forgive the person who offends you. Remember the Lord forgave you, so you must forgive others. And the most important piece of clothing you must wear is love. Love is what binds us all together in perfect harmony." (Colossians 3:12-14)

7. *Respond to the Holy Spirit.* Be willing to respond to the Holy Spirit's prompting and take the action steps wherever you are directed, such as prayer and fasting; attending a deliverance ministry, retreat, or prophetic conference; Bible study; Scripture mediation; listening to specific Christian music, teaching, or preaching; and/or praying and confessing with another believer. The Holy Spirit knows exactly what you need, when you need it and how you need it, to set you completely free.

"However, this kind does not go out except by prayer and fasting." (Matthew 17:21 NKJV)

"Confess your trespasses to one another, and pray for one another, that you may be healed. The effective, fervent prayer of a righteous man avails much." (James 5:16 NKJV)

8. *Pray for self-deliverance.* This is casting out demons from yourself. There are many resources of prayers, confessions, renunciations, and casting out demons that you can find in books and online. The resources that are being referenced here are listed on the reference page.

> *Prayer: Father, I come humbly before You and ask for You to forgive me for my sin and alignment with demonic forces and the generations before me. I ask that You cancel all ground that has allowed demonic forces to gain a foothold in my life. I bind every demonic strong man that has gained entry into my life, in the name of Jesus, and command all of them to come up and out in Jesus' name. Amen!*

- Confess and renounce: Confess every direct sin and generational sin that you may be aware of or that the Holy Spirit reveals to you. Key confessions include sins of idolatry; disobedience; pride; rebellion; Jezebel-controlling; manipulation and seduction; practices with the occult (horoscope and psychic reading); all inherited unrepented sin from the occult; sexual perversion; lust; masturbation; adultery and homosexuality, unforgiveness to someone who abandoned or abused you; trauma of rejection; false religions; ungodly soul ties with any person from your family, friends, or past relationships; curses spoken over yourself by you or from someone else; addictions; fears and phobias; and anything else that is sin in your life. Then renounce ever going back to that sin and behavior. For example: *Heavenly Father, I profess Jesus is my Lord and Savior, and I am sorry for the sin of idolatry and following false religions in my life and ask that You forgive me. I forgive those who were involved in introducing me to the false religions, including the leaders who impacted my life. I will never go back and renounce this now, in the name of Jesus!* Repeat for every confessed sin.

- Pray and ask God to cancel ground in every area where demons have been controlling and have access to you. Only God has the ultimate authority to forgive sin and cancel the ground that has been surrendered to demons; man does not. Sample prayer: *Father, I come humbly before You and ask that You would cancel the ground any demons have had in my life. I ask this in the name of Jesus!*

- Command and cast the demons out. For example: *I command you, demon of control, idolatry, fear to come up and out in the name of Jesus. Leave me now and never come back. Go out into the abyss.* Don't argue, talk to, or entertain the demons. Stand in your authority in Christ to cast them out! Repeat for every sin area.

"Look, I [Jesus] have given you authority over all the power of the enemy, and you can walk among snakes and scorpions and crush them. Nothing will injure you." (Luke 10:19-20 NLT)

HOMEWORK AND DISCUSSION

1. What limitations does the secular health community have in complete healing of the mind and emotions?

2. What does the Christian community provide for healing?

3. What has the power to restart the brain and transform a person's mind?

4. What must we discover about ourselves for deliverance from a dysfunctional soul?

5. How do we break free from a dysfunctional soul developed in our childhood?

Take time to reflect and share what you just learned and any experiences as the Holy Spirit leads.

CHAPTER SIX

TRANSFORMING YOUR MIND

HOW DO YOU transform your mind?

"Don't copy the behavior and customs of this world, but let God transform you into a new person by changing the way you think. Then you will know what God wants you to do, and you will know how good and pleasing and perfect His will really is." (Romans 12:2 NIV)

We learned in chapter two about three places where we have a mind: the head, the heart, and the gut. We also learned that our memories are distributed in our organs throughout our body. Memories of everything we've learned, experienced, watched, and/or sensed are stored in our mind. The sin nature we were born with as described by Jesus in the Bible also resides in our mind, along with behaviors we've developed, good and bad.

In order to transform our mind, we must deliberately change what we put in our mind. What we put in our thalamus (our mind's hard drive) will result in changing what comes out. Imagine your thalamus as an existing filing cabinet where you store old and new files. You can only go back and pull out of that filing cabinet what is in it. Likewise, you can only pull out of your mind what is there. If you want good things out, you must put good things in and focus your thoughts, as revealed in the Scripture.

> "Finally, brethren, whatsoever things are true, whatsoever things are honest, whatsoever things are just, whatsoever things are pure, whatsoever things are lovely, whatsoever things are of good report; if there be any virtue, and if there be any praise, think on these things." (Philippians 4:8 KJV)

Several keys to transforming your mind are praying the Word, knowing God's Word, hearing God's Word, surrender and sanctification to the work of the Holy Spirit, and doing life with other believers.

PRAYING THE WORD

God answers prayer in line with His Word and will for your life. It says that God is looking to and fro for a heart who is seeking Him. When you sincerely pray and ask the Lord to transform your mind and heart to align with His will, He will do it. Chapter eight will discuss this in more detail. A good Scripture to pray daily for transformation is Psalm 139:23-24.

> "Search me, O God and know my heart; test me and know my anxious thoughts. Point out anything in me that offends you and lead me along the path of everlasting life." (Psalm 139:23-24 NLT)

Ask the Holy Spirit to lead you to specific prayers for you.

KNOWING GOD'S WORD

Reading and studying the Holy Bible is critical for your growth and transformation into God's plan for your life. Knowing the Bible and memorizing Scripture like you would study in school to pass a test or class is critical. As you learn the Word of God and how to apply it to your everyday life, you will begin to discover truths that you otherwise would not know. As the Scripture says:

> "All scripture is inspired by God and is useful to teach us what is true and to make us realize what is wrong in our lives. It straightens us out and teaches us to do what is right. It is God's way of preparing us in every way, fully equipped for every good thing God wants us to do." (2 Timothy 3:16-17 NIV)

When we really see ourselves in light of the Word of God, we will stop pointing the finger at others and acknowledge our innate sin nature with the only antidote being the shed blood of Jesus Christ! We deceive ourselves when we look at someone else's bad behavior and think, "Thank God I'm not like them." As the Scripture reveals:

> "When they refused to acknowledge God, he abandoned them to their evil minds, and let them do things that should never be done. Their lives became full of every kind of wickedness, sin, greed, hate, envy, murder, fighting, deception, malicious behavior and gossip. They are backstabbers, haters of God, insolent, proud, and boastful. They are forever inventing new ways of sinning and are disobedient to their parents. They refuse to understand, break their promises, and are heartless and unforgiving. They are fully aware of God's death penalty for those who do such things, yet they go right ahead and do them anyway. And worse yet, they encourage others to do them too. You may be saying, 'What terrible people you have been talking about!' But you are just as bad, and you have no excuse! When you say they are wicked and should be punished, you are condemning yourself, for you do these very same things." (Romans 1:28-2:1 NLT)

The Bible is clear: we all have sinned and fallen short of

God's glory. It may just manifest in a different way from one person to another, but at our core is a sinful nature.

> "For everyone has sinned; we all fall short of God's glorious standard." (Romans 3:23 NLT)

Trauma in our life can be used as an excuse to cover sinful behavior. But when the trauma is healed and the demons are cast out, we are still left with a sin nature that has to be transformed if we want God's will for our life.

So, to be transformed from ungodly to godly behavior, reading and meditating on God's Word, allowing it to get in us, allows us to act on it rather than our sin nature when circumstances and situations arise. Get up preferably early in the morning and read your Bible, whether your flesh wants to or not. Take authority over your flesh and make yourself do it. Read the Old Testament and the New Testament.

> "Jesus Christ is the same yesterday, today and always." (Hebrews 12:8 NKJV)

Ask the Holy Spirit to guide you in your reading. The Holy Spirit will lead you right where you need to be reading for your personal spiritual growth. As you are reading, when Scripture is illuminated–when it jumps out at you off of the page or leaves an impression in your mind and heart–write it down on a piece of paper or 3 x 5 card, or type it in your iPad or phone notes. Include the date as a spiritual marker. Read the Scripture daily. Memorize it and get it in your mind. Ask the Holy Spirit to give you understanding and revelation of what you are to receive from the particular Scripture.

HEARING GOD'S WORD

Speak the Word to your mind over and over again until it becomes a part of you, especially in an area that you are trying to overcome. In my research, I learned that speaking the Word out loud to our mind is very receptive in the transformation process, as your mind is most receptive to your own voice. Also, attend a Bible-believing and Holy Spirit-led church. Listen to prophetic preaching and teaching as led by the Holy Spirit and confirm what you're hearing with the Word.

> "So then, faith comes by hearing, and hearing by the Word of God." (Romans 10:17 NKJV)

As you listen to preachers, television, radio, or social media ministries, ask the Holy Spirit for discernment and clarity in your hearing.

When you listen to a transforming word from a man or woman of God called to preach or teach the gospel, you should receive one or more of the following: confirmation, conviction, or deliverance.

- Confirmation of where the Holy Spirit has been leading in your reading.

- Conviction to turn away from sin that you've been ignoring, denying, or just now recognizing.

- Deliverance from mental strongholds and lies you've believed, whether of the flesh, the world, demonic oppression, or demonization that have kept you from receiving the truth in a particular area in your life.

The Word is alive and powerful to change who you are from the inside out.

> "For the Word of God is living and powerful, and sharper than any two-edged sword, piercing even to the division of soul and spirit, and of joints and marrow, and is a discerner of the thoughts and intents of the heart." (Hebrews 4:12 NKJV)

SURRENDER AND SANCTIFICATION

As you surrender your life to the Lordship of Jesus Christ, circumstances in your life to separate you from sin in line with the Word you are reading, studying, and/or receiving will emerge and the Holy Spirit will guide you through. This process is described in the Bible as sanctification. It is a "spiritual surgery." The degree to which you cooperate with the Holy Spirit will be the deciding factor on receiving complete transformation in a particular area or issue the Lord is dealing with in your life. This is only a spiritual work performed by God alone and cannot be performed by a doctor or surgeon.

We need to understand sin and why we need to be separated from it.

What is sin? Sin is not a mistake, or accident, or failure. Sin is an act of the will through disobedience to the one true God of the Bible, whether done deliberately or in ignorance or minimizing it. Sin is rebellion against God's will and plan for our life. It is choosing our own way. Every sin committed in the natural can be linked to an affront to God. For instance, spending your life building your kingdom versus God's kingdom in your church, business, or family can be linked to pride, selfish ambition, or rebellion—or all three.

The Bible tells us we are all born with an evil nature. This is the human condition. Sanctification separates us from our natural inclination toward sin. When we cooperate with the sanctification process of the Holy Spirit, we move from being led by our flesh to being led by the Spirit.

> "If your sinful nature controls your mind, there is death. But if the Holy Spirit controls your mind, there is life and peace." (Romans 8:6 NLT)

God will allow circumstances to arise in your life that will trigger your mind's unconscious stored defense mechanisms to surface in order to deliver you from its bondage.

As an example, God will allow circumstances to align in your life to deliver you from rejection in your mind which was not properly processed or released. Your mind may send signals through chemical impulses in your brain that current events similar to something traumatic in your past requires you to take action. Your stored defense mechanism may have been to lash out, ignore its reality, flee the situation, and/or respond with rejection.

When you submit to the Lordship of Jesus Christ, He will do a work in you which can only be done supernaturally! When you apply the truth, knowing who you are in Christ–that God's love for you was so great, Jesus died on the cross so you could live with God for eternity–you cancel rejection's power over you! When you accept the truth of who you are apart from Christ along with every other person, all falling short of the glory of God, then you will see the person rejecting you as simply acting out of their own spiritual condition. Finally, when you act on the truth and offer forgiveness, you receive forgiveness and allow the Lord to move you into greater faith from glory to glory.

As you apply these truths, new neurons and habits will form in your mind and you will be released from the wrong mindset that held you captive whenever you experienced rejection.

> "The Spirit of the Lord is upon Me, because He
> has anointed Me to preach the gospel to the poor;
> He has sent Me to heal the brokenhearted, to
> proclaim liberty to the captives and recovery of
> sight to the blind, to set at liberty those who are
> oppressed." (Luke 4:18 NKJV)

LIVING LIFE WITH OTHER BELIEVERS

There are multiple Scriptures that emphasize the need to be in relationship with other believers. As we walk through transformation and sanctification, it may be another believer that brings a word to open our spiritual eyes to understand what the Holy Spirit is doing.

> "As iron sharpens iron, so one person sharpens another." (Proverbs 27:17 NIV)

We need each other to walk this spiritual journey. God did not create us to walk with Him alone, but with other brothers and sisters in Christ.

> "Two are better than one, because they have a good return for their labor: If either of them falls down, one can help the other up. But pity anyone who falls and has no one to help them up. Also, if two lie down together, they will keep warm. But how can one keep warm alone? Though one may be overpowered, two can defend themselves. A cord of three strands is not quickly broken." (Ecclesiastes 4:9-12 NIV)

So community is not only for sharpening one another, but also for standing through the trials and temptations that invariably come our way. Another believer may be able to see what you cannot see and bring light to your situation.

> "For the weapons of our warfare are not carnal

but mighty in God for pulling down strongholds, casting down arguments and every high thing that exalts itself against the knowledge of God, bringing every thought into captivity to the obedience of Christ." (2 Corinthians 10:4-5 NKJV)

In addition, the gospel is free and so is everything else we need for complete wholeness! You can't afford a psychologist? Go see a sister or brother in Christ that you're walking in unity with and counsel each other.

"Let the message about Christ, in all its richness, fill your lives. Teach and counsel each other with all the wisdom he gives. Sing psalms and hymns and spiritual songs to God with thankful hearts." (Colossians 3:16 NLT)

HOMEWORK AND DISCUSSION SESSION

1. What are the keys to transforming your mind?

2. Which key would you consider the most important in transforming your mind?

3. Why do we even want to transform our mind?

4. What is the Holy Spirit's role in transforming your mind?

Begin to speak Scripture to your mind as led by the Holy Spirit. When circumstances arise, respond according to

Scripture and not how your sinful nature or your brain was previously programmed to respond.

Share a mind transforming example.

KNOW WHO YOU ARE IN CHRIST

I. Believe the Word about your new identity in Christ:

Question 1: Are you a sinner in Christ? Or are you righteous in Christ?

Answer: _____
_____
_____
_____
_____

Give the Scripture verses you're using to support your answer and explain why you believe it.

Question 2: Does committing sin disqualify you as righteous in Christ? Yes or no?

Answer: _____

_____

_____

_____

_____

Give an example to support your answer and the Scripture verses.

Question 3: Contrast your old identity with your new identity according to Scripture and share examples.

OLD NATURE	NEW NATURE
_____	_____
_____	_____
_____	_____
_____	_____
_____	_____
_____	_____
_____	_____
_____	_____
_____	_____

II. Sanctification and walking in newness of life:

Question 4: What is the key to living out your new identity in Christ?

Answer: _____

_____

_____

_____

_____

1. Believe what the Word says about you and your new life in Christ.

2. Walk after the Spirit.

3. Don't mind the things of the flesh. When the Holy Spirit points out/convicts of sin, repent and move on.

List Scriptures that come to mind that correspond to each item above:

1. _____

2. _____

3. _____

Question 5: How do you separate yourself from the sin in your life?

Answer: Allow the work of the Holy Spirit through sanctification to separate you unto holiness.

> "Work out your own salvation with fear and trembling; for it is God who works in you both to will and to do for His good pleasure." (Philippians 2:12b-13 NKJV)

_____

_____

_____

_____

Write the Scripture verses to support the above.

If the Lord revealed all of our sin to us at once, our flesh would not be able to handle it. Therefore, like children growing and learning from infancy through adulthood, the Holy Spirit guides us into all truth about ourselves, the world, and the enemy.

As we receive these truths, reject lies, and turn away from our old nature (sinful behaviors and habits), we will begin discovering our spiritual DNA along the path the Lord designed uniquely for us. We are held accountable for what we know as the Holy Spirit reveals.

Resource for finding Scriptures: Ask the Holy Spirit to lead you to the Scriptures. You can use www.blueletterbible.org for online scripture search.

CHAPTER EIGHT

PRAY AND PRAISE ABOUT EVERYTHING

I N THE COURSE of the day, you can speak to God anytime and anywhere: with your eyes open or shut, standing up, driving in your car, or kneeling down. God is with you and wants to be a part of your everyday life, even in the minor details. You can speak to God in any language: English, German, Spanish, or your spiritual language.

When you pray according to God's Word, you will experience the hand of God in your life. Pray to have your spiritual eyes open and your ears receptive to what the Spirit is saying to you. When you pray in the Holy Spirit, you build your inner man.

"But you, dear friends, must build each other up

in your most holy faith, pray in the power of the Holy Spirit..." (Jude 1:20 NLT)

PRAYING ACCORDING TO GOD'S WORD FOR WISDOM

When you need wisdom, talk to God and go to God first.

> "If you need wisdom—if you want to know what God wants you to do—ask him, and he will gladly tell you. He will not resent your asking. But when you ask him, be sure that you really expect him to answer, for a doubtful mind is as unsettled as a wave of the sea that is driven and tossed by the wind. That man should not think he will receive anything from the Lord; he is a double-minded man, unstable in all he does." (James 1:5-8 NLT)

If you're praying continuously and not receiving wisdom from the Lord according to James 1: 5-8, ask the Lord to reveal what is preventing you from receiving an answer.

In the previous chapter, arrested development/fixation was defined. The following symptoms could be one of the factors preventing you from receiving wisdom from the Lord:

1. *Defies authority:* You defy authority because the authority in your life didn't protect or provide or couldn't read your mind to help you with your conflict resolution or keep you safe. Therefore, you become your own authority.

2. *Loss of value:* You automatically lose your self-value system. You believe you're defective and flawed. You feel or become powerless (targets, victims). Children take 100% responsibility for all losses and traumas (i.e. if mom or dad dies, the child thinks, "What could I have done differently so she or he would have lived?")

3. *Loss of trust:* You don't trust anyone, not even yourself.

4. *Doubt truth and fear knowledge:* You don't want to know the facts or what could be wrong with you and you don't believe it when it's pointed out to you.

When you receive an answer from the Holy Spirit, do whatever He tells you to do. Nothing more or nothing less. Be obedient.

PRAYING ACCORDING TO GOD'S WORD FOR YOUR NEEDS

"But my God shall supply all your needs according to his riches in glory by Christ Jesus." (Philippians 4:19 KJV)

Lord, Your Word says that You will supply all of my needs. Right now, Lord, this is what I believe I need: _____. And I'm trusting You to supply my need. If there is something else that I need, reveal it to me, Holy Spirit, so I can line my thinking up to what You know I really need according to the Word. I lift this prayer up to You, in Jesus' name.

Sometimes we think we know what we need. It seems clear: a little more money in the bank account, more vacation time, less stress. But the truth is, God knows exactly what we need. It could be to trust Him more, to know the peace that surpasses all understanding in Christ Jesus regardless of the circumstances, or to turn away from behaviors that are not leading to life. Whatever it is, God knows, and the Bible tells us that the Spirit intercedes on our behalf for what we really need:

> "In the same way, the Spirit helps us in our weakness. We do not know what we ought to pray for, but the Spirit himself intercedes for us through wordless groans." (Romans 8:26 NIV)

Continue to pray for your needs to be met, and be open to the Lord answering your prayer in ways you were not expecting. When you receive the answer, embrace it and be obedient to the leading of the Holy Spirit, knowing that God knows what you really need. Remember, the Lord will not bring anything into your life that does not line up with His Word.

RECITING AND MEDITATING ON SCRIPTURES RECEIVED FROM THE HOLY SPIRIT

Whatever specific need you believe you have, pray for the Holy Spirit to lead you to the Scriptures that you should be praying. As He reveals them to you, write them down and write your own prayer and confess it over your life out loud. Speak it to your brain and heart to absorb this truth until you have a breakthrough.

This could include needs for increasing your faith, mental and emotional healing, improving your finances, your love walk, forgiving others, accepting authority, having a teachable spirit, trusting, accepting knowledge, taking authority over your thought life, turning away from a specific sinful behavior, and any others the Holy Spirit brings to your memory.

Pray according to God's Word for knowing what God's will is and to have the wisdom and understanding to carry it out.

> "For this reason, since the day we heard about you, we have not stopped praying for you and asking God to fill you with the knowledge of his will, through all spiritual wisdom and understanding. And we pray this in order that you may live a life worthy of the Lord and may please him in every way: bearing fruit in every good work, growing in the knowledge of God, being strengthened with all power according to his glorious might so that you may have great endurance and patience, and joyfully giving thanks to the Father, who has qualified you to share in the inheritance of the saints in the kingdom of light." (Colossians 1:9-12 NIV)

This Scripture says it all:

- fill you with knowledge of His will

- through all spiritual wisdom and understanding

- live a life worthy of the Lord

- please Him in every way

- bearing fruit in every good work

- growing in the knowledge of God

- being strengthened with all power with His glorious might

- have great endurance and patience

- joyfully giving thanks to the Father for qualifying you.

Write your own prayer using this Scripture and begin to confess it over your life, speaking it out loud to your brain and heart. Also, write a prayer for your brothers and sisters in Christ whom the Holy Spirit places on your heart. Pray for them and share this prayer with others as you are led.

PRAISE GOD ALWAYS

Praise is a powerful spiritual key you can use to cause the enemy to flee from your life. Praise is warfare against everything the devil is trying to bring against you. A spirit of heaviness is emotional and mental oppression from the devil, which can be in the form of depression, grief, discouragement, loss, thoughts of suicide, etc.

Jesus came to set us free from this.

> "The Spirit of the Sovereign Lord is upon me, because the Lord has appointed me to bring good news to the poor. He has sent me to bind up the brokenhearted, to proclaim freedom for the captives and release from darkness for the prisoners... to bestow on them a crown of beauty, instead of ashes, the oil of joy instead of mourning, and a garment of praise, instead of a spirit of despair." (Isaiah 61:1-3 NIV)

According to the Scripture, praise is a garment, so we need to put it on. It's a choice we make. We should put on praise every day! Praise the Lord no matter what is going on around you. Praise changes everything.

Praise brings joy into your life regardless of the circumstances, good or bad.

> "Enter his gates with thanksgiving and his courts with praise; give thanks to Him and praise his name." (Psalm 100:4 NIV)

> "Be anxious for nothing but in everything by prayer and petition with thanksgiving..." (Philippians 4:6-7 NLT)

"Give thanks in all circumstances for this is God's will for you in Christ Jesus." (1 Thessalonians 5:18 NIV)

Share a praise experience.

CHAPTER NINE

WALK BY FAITH AND LOVE

I. Walk by Faith:

What is faith? According to Scripture:

> "It is the confident assurance that what we hope for is going to happen. It is the evidence of things we cannot see." (Hebrews 11:1 NLT)

What do you think of when you read this Scripture? List what comes to your mind.

_____

_____

_____

_____

Have you experienced the fulfillment of this Scripture in your life? If so, how?

_____

_____

_____

_____

What are we instructed to do in the Word when what we're believing for by faith has yet to manifest in the natural? List Scriptures that the Holy Spirit brings to mind.

_____

_____

_____

_____

How do we obtain faith?

_____

_____

_____

"Yet faith comes from listening to this message of good news–the Good News about Christ." (Romans 10:17 NLT)

"So, then faith comes by hearing, and hearing by the word of God." (Romans 10:17 NKJV)

What do we need faith for? (Find the Scripture reference for each below.)

1. Salvation. _____

2. To be declared righteous before God. _____

3. To believe God's Word. _____

4. To please and honor God. _____

5. To walk in the Spirit. _____

Select one of the above to focus on and share your thoughts within group time. Write any notes below.

II. Walk by Love:

When the Holy Spirit controls our lives, according to Galatians 5:20, He will produce the following in us:

Love, joy, peace, patience, kindness, goodness, faithfulness, gentleness, and self-control.

What is love?

> "Love is patient and kind. Love is not jealous or boastful or proud or rude. Love does not demand its own way. Love is not irritable, and it keeps no record of when it has been wronged. It is never glad about injustice but rejoices whenever the truth wins out. Love never gives up, never loses faith, is always hopeful, and endures through every circumstance.... Three things will last forever—faith, hope, and love—and the greatest of these is love." (1 Corinthians 13:4-7, 13 NLT)

What are the two greatest commandments Jesus gave us?

> "Jesus replied, "'Love the Lord your God with all your heart and with all your soul and with all your mind." This is the first and greatest commandment. And the second is like it: "Love your neighbor as yourself.""" (Matthew 22:37-39 NIV)

How do we walk in this kind of love?

_____

_____

_____

_____

"For this is the love of God, that we keep His commandments." (1 John 5:3a NKJV)

ESTABLISHING BOUNDARIES IN LOVE

Seek the Word and the Holy Spirit's guidance to establish healthy boundaries in your life and relationships.

You have control over what you allow to enter your life and how you react to what happens to you. From the things you say and do, people you let in, places you go, things you listen to, watch and participate in... to how you use your gifts for Kingdom purpose, such as your talents, finances, influences, skills, spiritual giftings.

If you are not affecting your world for Kingdom purpose, but are being infected with sin by it, then a boundary is needed.

Search the Scriptures for the following areas in which to establish boundaries:

- Yourself: The only effective boundaries you can place

are around yourself. Such as, what you will allow and not allow and where you will invest your time, energy, resources, and finances.

  ○ Psalm 1:1 (NKJV)
  ○ James 3:2 (NLT)

- Intimate relationship: spouse.
  ○ Matthew 19:5 (NKJV)

- Other relationships (family/friends): children, parents, extended family, best friends, boyfriend/girlfriend, boss, leaders, pastors, co-workers, brothers and sisters in Christ.
  ○ 1 Peter 4:8 (NIV)
  ○ Matthew 18:15 (NLT)
  ○ 1 Corinthians 5:9-10 (NLT)

GROUP DISCUSSION: SHARE OTHER SCRIPTURES

A boundary prayer:

> *Father God, if there is no Kingdom purpose, please close this door (to this situation, people, place, or thing) and lock it; otherwise, please give me the grace to walk through it. In Jesus' name, I pray, amen.*

WALK BY FAITH AND LOVE THROUGH OBEDIENCE AND FORGIVENESS

Your obedience to God indicates your love for Him by faith.

To honor God is to love others in spite of how they treat you (you can love from a distance if the relationship is abusive/toxic).

When you are walking in faith and love, you rise above the circumstances that surround you. Your love is based on what God says for you to do in His Word, not on your feelings or emotions. Honoring God means to obey Him regardless of your feelings or emotions.

For example, "I love you because God commanded me to, not based on how I feel."

- There can't be love where there is no obedience.

- There is no love where there is no honor.

- It's a dishonor for you to have strife with someone in your life.

- Honor rises above hurt and pain.

Forgiveness is a Kingdom key which sets you free to discover your spiritual DNA. It releases you from the bondage of mental strongholds.

You're stuck where you are unless you get past unforgiveness.

Every attack by the enemy against you is designed to attack your relationship with God as it relates to your love walk. It is designed to keep you from discovering your spiritual DNA.

Below is a daily confession, taken from a pastor who went through a horrific event of the murder of his pregnant wife:

Today I am deciding to love not hate.

Today I am deciding to extend forgiveness not bitterness.

Today I am deciding to hope not despair.

By Jesus' power at work within us, the best is STILL yet to come.

Even when I don't see it, I believe it to be true....

CHAPTER TEN

GOD'S SOVEREIGNTY AND SPIRITUAL BATTLES

GOD'S SOVEREIGNTY

"Remember it is better to suffer for doing good, if that is what God wants, than to suffer for doing wrong!" (I Peter 3:17 NLT)

SUFFERING AND TRIALS allowed by God brings deliverance and increases faith and trust in God. It's a bondage breaker. It brings about transformation in our inner life that only God can do, changing us from the inside out.

Suffering for doing wrong is a consequence of behavior, which may bring about an outward change, but has no effect on changing who we are on the inside.

Whenever God through the Holy Spirit is drawing you toward your destiny, spiritual warfare is eminent. God's sovereignty is to develop character in you to be more like Jesus and fulfill your God-given purpose. The enemy's tactics working with your flesh is to interfere and stop God's plan.

The questions you will need to ask during these difficult times are:

- God, is this Your sovereign hand in my life?
  - If so, then help me, Lord, to be still, knowing that the battle belongs to You!

- Or is this the enemy trying to block my way or pull me back to keep me bound?

- Or is this my flesh, my subconscious mind, or unconscious defense mechanism and developed habits that's fighting to keep me in my comfort zone?
  - If it's either the enemy or my flesh, lead me, Holy Spirit, to use the spiritual keys given in the Scriptures to bind the enemy and loose truth over the lies in my mind to bring down the strongholds. Pray and confess Matthew 16:19 and 2 Corinthians 10:3-6.

DISCERNMENT

Discernment comes from being well versed in the Word and reliant on the Holy Spirit. In order to be able to discern between right and wrong, truth and lies, good and evil, you must be reliant on the Holy Spirit and the Word. You need both! The Holy Spirit will lead and guide you into all truth. As the Scriptures say:

> "When the Spirit of truth comes, he will guide you into all truth. He will not be presenting his own ideas; he will be telling you what he has heard. He will tell you about the future." (John 16:13 NLT)

> "Everyone has heard about your obedience, so I rejoice because of you; but I want you to be wise about what is good, and innocent about what is evil." (Romans 16:19 NIV)

> "For everything that is hidden or secret will eventually be brought to light and made plain to all. So be sure to pay attention to what you hear. To those who are open to my teaching, more understanding will be given. But to those who are not listening, even what they think they have will be taken away from them." (Luke 8:17-18 NLT)

> "Behold, I send you out as sheep in the midst of wolves. Therefore, be wise as serpents and harmless as doves." (Matthew 10:16 NKJV)

As you are yielded to the leading of the Holy Spirit, He will guide and lead you to or away from people, circumstances, and situations where you should or should not be. Having keen discernment in reliance on the Holy Spirit and the Word of God will guide you through all spiritual battles that come your way.

SPIRITUAL BATTLES

We are in a spiritual battle every day of our lives, whether we know it or not. Spiritual battles come in all shapes and sizes. For this study, we will focus on three kinds of spiritual battles–minor, major, and severe–and our responses to them.

1. *Minor battles:* These could be referred to as the battle of the tongue.

    "We all make many mistakes, but those who control their tongues can also control themselves in every other way." (James 3:2 NLT)

    "Keep your lips from speaking evil, keep your tongues from telling lies." (1 Peter 3:10 NLT)

List other spiritual battles that come to your mind that fall in the minor battles category.

_____

_____

_____

_____

2. *Major battles:* These spiritual battles require more discernment from the Holy Spirit and hearing from God and often include overcoming strongholds.

    The question you might ask is, "God, is this You closing the door or is this the enemy trying to stop me from moving forward?"

How do you know when you've heard from God?

First, know that God speaks through His Word. The Holy Spirit will lead you to scriptures that will speak to you.

   "To keep me from becoming conceited because of these surpassingly great revelations, there was given me a thorn in my flesh, a messenger from Satin, to torment me. Three times I pleaded with the Lord to take it away from me. But he said to me, 'My Grace is sufficient for you, for my power is made perfect in weakness.' Therefore, I will boast all the more gladly about my weaknesses, so that Christ's power may rest on me." (1 Corinthians 12:7 NIV)

Second, fight the good fight of faith. This means doing nothing when you have the power to do something, but God tells you not to.

"Be still, and know that I am God." (Psalm 46:10 NIV)

"Not by might, nor by power, but by my Spirit, says the Lord Almighty." (Zechariah 4:6 NIV)

Third, look for confirmation. Wait until you've received confirmation from two or three witnesses. Holy Spirit confirmation can come in the form of peace about a situation and "lighting up" Scripture during your reading time.

When you're arrested in development, one of the symptoms is loss of impulse control. Waiting on God develops the fruit of the spirit of patience in us, rewiring our brains to overcome the impulse control that drives our behavior, which acts out of fleshly desires from what was stored and embedded in our mind's thalamus.

List spiritual battles that come to your mind that may fall in the major battle category.

_____

_____

_____

_____

3. *Severe battles:* These battles come to test who you are in Christ! They will test your faith at the highest level.

Give some examples of severe spiritual battles either from experience or from the Word.

Some biblical examples of severe spiritual battles: The lives of Job; Joseph; Shadrach, Meshach, and Abednego; and Jesus.

"Thou he slay me, yet will I hope in him." (Job 13:15 NLT)

"'Please, come closer,' he said to them. So they came closer. And he said again, 'I am Joseph, your brother, whom you sold into slavery in Egypt. But don't be upset, and don't be angry with yourselves for selling me to this place. It was God who sent me here ahead of you to preserve your lives.'" (Genesis 45:4-5 NLT)

"If we are thrown into the blazing furnace, the God whom we serve is able to save us. He will rescue us from your power, Your Majesty. But even if he doesn't, Your Majesty, you can be sure that we will never serve your gods or worship the gold statue you have set up." (Daniel 3:17-18 NIV)

"Going a little further, he fell with his face to the ground and prayed, 'My Father, if it be possible, may this cup be taken from me. Yet not as I will, but as you will.'" (Matthew 26:39 NIV)

What is the common thread in the biblical examples above?

RESPONSES TO SPIRITUAL BATTLES

"We can rejoice, too, when we run into problems and trials, for we know that they help us develop endurance. And endurance develops strength of character, and character strengthens our confident hope of salvation." (Romans 5:3-4 NLT)

Review and write supporting Scriptures and examples that come to mind for group discussion below.

_____

_____

_____

_____

• Praise the Lord. Praising the Lord is therapeutic.

"Give thanks in all circumstances for this is God's will for you in Christ Jesus." (1 Thessalonians 5:17 NLT)

• Pray Scripture and pray in the Spirit.

"Assuredly, I say to you, whatever you bind on earth will be bound in heaven, and whatever you loose on earth will be loosed in heaven. Again,

I say to you that if two of you agree on earth concerning anything that they ask, it will be done for them by My Father in heaven." (Matthew 18:18-19 NKJV)

- Pray and fast: bringing down strongholds and casting out demonic influences.

  "For though we live in the world, we do not wage war as the world does. The weapons we fight with are not the weapons of the world. On the contrary, they have divine power to demolish strongholds." (2 Corinthians 10:3-4 NIV)

- Confess the Word over yourself and your situation. Find Scriptures that encourage you, where the Holy Spirit leads and speaks to your circumstance. The Word is medicine. It is alive.

  "It is written, Man does not live by bread alone, but by every word that proceeded out of the mouth of God." (Matthew 4:4 KJV)

- Listen to the Word preached: local church, television, radio, app, CDs, etc. as led by the Holy Spirit.

- Sing songs of worship.

- Weep and cry out to God.

  "Weeping may endure for a night, but joy cometh

in the morning." (Psalm 30:5 KJV)

VICTORY OVER SPIRITUAL BATTLES

The enemy's intent according to Scripture is to kill, steal, and destroy (see John 10:10). He is out to destroy our relationship first with God and then with those around us.

God's intent is to transform us into the likeness of Jesus. To develop our character to stand firm on the truth, no matter what comes against us. To grow in the knowledge of God. To build our faith. To trust God in every circumstance of our life.

God uses spiritual battles to deliver us from strongholds that keep us in bondage and immobilized. Some spiritual battles are going to take you back to the place where you were wounded and the stronghold was established, which usually occurred in early childhood. While this may be painful, keep in mind the Holy Spirit will not reveal what you cannot handle or ask you to revisit what is not necessary for your healing.

If you are aware of being arrested in development, when you are in the battle, start to discern and ask yourself, "Is this a true emotion or a perceived one from my inner child's point of view? Is this a deception from the enemy attacking my childlike emotions?" Either way, do what the Word tells you to do and as the Holy Spirit guides.

"For God has not given us a spirit of fear and

timidity, but of power, love and self-discipline." (2 Timothy 1:7 NLT)

Overcoming spiritual battles brings freedom from the former authorities in our life: the flesh, the world, and the enemy.

There are numerous Scriptures that speak to spiritual battles and God's purpose for them in the life of a believer. List one or more to share in group discussion.

_____

_____

_____

_____

DAILY PRAYER RECOMMENDATION FOR DELIVERANCE FROM STRONGHOLDS

"Search me, God, and know my heart; test me and know my anxious thoughts. See if there is any offensive way in me, and lead me in the way everlasting." (Psalm 139:23-24 NLT)

Note: When all hell has come against you; it's reassuring to know that God is in it, using it for your good and walking through it with you. (See Romans 8:28.)

The Word of God is clear: we overcome by the blood of the Lamb and the Word of our testimony:

> "And they overcame him by the blood of the Lamb,
> and by the Word of their testimony; and they
> loved not their lives unto the death." (Revelation
> 12:11 KJV)

I went through my own tribulation for a period of seven years. This was after signing up for my first Bible study. It was then that Satan and his cohorts woke up and the war against my mind and soul was on in the attempt to keep me from pursuing discovering my own spiritual DNA. It was the Word of God strapped around me like a parachute and following the leading of the Holy Spirit that brought me through and why I'm still here today!

GUARD YOUR HEART

When battles have subsided, remember to guard your heart.

> "Above all else, guard your heart, for it affects
> everything you do." (Proverbs 4:23 NLT)

The devil would love to pull you back into the bondage from which you've been delivered. He can only do this through deception, but as you stay connected to the Holy Spirit and obeying the Word, you will be victorious through Christ.

> "Jesus said to the people who believed in him,
> 'You are truly my disciples if you keep obeying my
> teachings. And you will know the truth and the

truth will set you free.'" (John 8:31-32 NLT)

ESCAPING TEMPTATION

Once a thought penetrates your mind, evaluate it on the basis of Philippians 4:8, which describes what we should think about: "whatever is true, honorable, right, pure, lovely, good report, any virtue, worthy of praise." Then ask yourself:

- Will this thought bring out the best in my life?

- Does it line up with God's Word?

- If this thought becomes an action, can it be used for Kingdom purposes?

- If the answer to any of these is "no," then you need to cast out the thought and think of something that will bring a "yes."

Even if you slip up, the Word, the Holy Spirit and the name of Jesus will deliver you out of it. Search the Scriptures. Pray and seek the Holy Spirit's guidance and godly counsel.

OPEN DISCUSSION

CHAPTER ELEVEN

DISCOVER YOUR SPIRITUAL DNA

YOUR SPIRITUAL DNA encompasses your:

1. spiritual gifts and personality traits

2. special abilities and talents

3. passion and desires of your heart

4. spiritual family's bloodline

5. anointing.

Kingdom Key: Only the Holy Spirit can reveal your spiritual DNA to you.

When you are operating in your spiritual DNA, you will have an internal knowledge that you are doing exactly what God designed uniquely for you to do for the advancement of the Kingdom. You will be inclined to do it by the prompting of the Holy Spirit moving you forward on your spiritual journey.

> "For all who are led by the Spirit of God are children of God." (Romans 8:14 NLT)

> "But the natural man does not receive the things of the Spirit of God, for they are foolishness to him; nor can he know them, because they are spiritually discerned." (1 Corinthians 2:14 NKJV)

YOUR SPIRITUAL DNA

Let's take a closer look at what our spiritual DNA encompasses.

1. Spiritual gifts and personality traits

You can take a spiritual gifting and personality trait assessment to learn what they are, make your own assessment, or ask the Holy Spirit.

A psychological theory suggests that there are four fundamental personality types or DISC temperaments and basic motivations:

- (D) Choleric (direct, decisive) - challenge and control

- (I) Sanguine (enthusiastic, active, social) - recognition and approval

- (S) Phlegmatic (relaxed, peaceful) - stability and support

- (C) Melancholic (analytical, wise, quiet) - quality and correctness

Spiritual gifting can be found in Romans 12:3-8, with this qualifier:

"For I say, through the grace given to me, to everyone who is among you, not to think of himself more highly than he ought to think, but to think soberly, as God has dealt to each one a measure of faith." (Romans 12:3 NKJV)

Spiritual gifting can also be found 1 Corinthians 12:27.

What are your spiritual gifts?

_____

_____

_____

_____

How did you learn these were your spiritual gifts?

_____

_____

_____

_____

2. Special abilities/talents and love language

You've known it forever, but can't quite put your finger on it. You ask yourself, "Why am I so good at this?" You dismiss it, and when you're walking in the natural, you use it to your advantage. This could be a special ability to draw people to you, to be believable, to inspire others. You can walk in a room and your presence screams "here I am" without saying a word. You have the answers to questions that others are still pondering. You're a fast learner. The list goes on. We all have them.

List some others:

_____

_____

_____

_____

Love languages are described as follows:

- encouraging words

- quality time

- acts of service

- gift giving

- physical touch

A clue to discovering which love language best describes you can be found by knowing which one you most likely give to your spouse or those you love. You can also take an online love language assessment.

Special abilities and talents are best realized as we begin experiencing our spiritual DNA emerge and God's intent for them.

What are your special abilities and talents that stand out from other people who may possess your similar spiritual gifts and personality traits?

_____

_____

_____

_____

3. Passions and desires of your heart

There are many things we can be passionate about, such as:

- a certain cause

- an industry

- a group

- a specialty

- a ministry

A doctor can be passionate about the heart. A dentist can be passionate about preventing cavities. An evangelist can be passionate about winning souls to Christ

You may find passions you once had have been buried. We serve a resurrecting God! As your spiritual DNA is discovered, those passions God put there initially will be resurrected. You will begin to experience them once again. Can you relate to this?

As you're operating in the Spirit, new passions and desires will enter your heart in line with Kingdom purposes. Have you had this experience?

What's the key to Discover your spiritual DNA and the desires of your heart?

> "Trust in the Lord, and do good; dwell in the land, and feed on His faithfulness. Delight yourself also in the Lord, And He shall give you the desires of your heart." (Psalm 37:3-4 NKJV)

OPEN DISCUSSION

4. Your spiritual family/bloodline

Embrace your spiritual family: your new bloodline.

When Jesus was speaking to the crowd, someone told Him His mother and brothers were outside and wanted to speak with Him. Although it was Mary who is highly favored by God, His natural mother, Jesus didn't jump up and rush to the door to let them in. Instead, according to Scripture:

> "Jesus asked, 'Who is my mother? Who are my brothers?' Then he pointed to his disciples and said, 'These are my mother and brothers. Anyone who does the will of my Father in heaven is my brother and sister and mother!'" (Matthew 12:48-49 NLT)

This is crucial because,

> "For the gifts and calling of God are without repentance." (Romans 11:29 KJV)

> "Not everyone who says to Me, 'Lord, Lord,' shall enter the kingdom of heaven, but he who does the will of My Father in heaven. Many will say to Me in that day, "Lord, Lord, have we not prophesied in Your name, cast out demons in Your name, and done many wonders in Your name? And then I will declare to them, "I never knew you;

depart from Me, you who practice lawlessness!"
(Matthew 7: 21-23 NKJV)

On another occasion, one of Jesus' disciples was posing the proposition that he would come back and follow Him, but first, he needed to go and bury his father. Jesus' reply:

"But Jesus said to him, 'Follow me, and let the dead bury their own dead.'" (Matthew 8:22 NKJV)

Jesus was establishing who our true family is in accordance with our spiritual DNA.

Where do you find your spiritual family? How do you decide what church to belong to? Are you embracing your natural or spiritual family? (Clue: with whom do you spend the majority of your time?)

Scriptures that speak to your spiritual family/bloodline include 1 Corinthians 12:13 and Romans 8:15. List others that come to mind.

_____

_____

_____

_____

5. Anointing

The anointing of God cannot be manufactured, it cannot be produced by human hands, it cannot be purchased, and it cannot be willed into your life. You cannot get it from a PhD in biblical studies and it doesn't come from gaining biblical knowledge.

The anointing of God comes from one place alone: when we have an authentic, surrendered relationship with Jesus and the Holy Spirit in accordance with God's Word.

Salvation is free. The anointing will cost you: dying to self, living for Christ, living holy as He is holy with fear of the Lord!

Jesus promised the Holy Spirit:

> "If you love me, obey my commandments. And I will ask the Father, and he will give you another counselor, who will never leave you. He is the Holy Spirit, who leads into all truth." (John 14:15-17a NLT)

> "John answered, saying to all, I indeed baptize you with water; but One mightier than I is coming, whose sandal strap I am not worthy to loose. He will baptize you with the Holy Spirit and fire." (Luke 3:16 NKJV)

> "Then there appeared to them divided tongues, as of fire, and one sat upon each of them. And they were all filled with the Holy Spirit and began to speak with other tongues, as the Spirit gave them utterance." (Acts 2:4b NKJV)

The anointing that comes from our relationship with the Holy Spirit is empowering, enabling, and elevating.

- <u>The anointing will empower you.</u> It will move you beyond your natural comfort zone to go where the Holy Spirit is leading and to do what you've been called to do. Paul had this pull, as he states:

  > "And now I am going to Jerusalem, drawn there by the Holy Spirit, not knowing what awaits me except that the Holy Spirit has told me in city after city that jail and suffering lie ahead. But my life is worth nothing unless I use it for doing the work assigned me by the Lord Jesus–the work of telling others the Good news about God's wonderful kindness and love." (Acts 20:22-24 NLT)

- <u>The anointing is a divine enabler.</u> It will enable you to do far more than you can do in the natural. The Holy Spirit reveals truths to you along your journey that you would not otherwise receive from any other source.

  > "But you have received the Holy Spirit, and he lives within you, so you don't need anyone to teach you what is true. For the Spirit teaches you everything

you need to know, and what he teaches is true–it is not a lie. So just as he has taught you, remain in fellowship with Christ." (1 John 2:27 NLT)

When you are operating in the anointing, you have power from God Almighty to transform lives and the only "degree" you need is from the University of the Holy Spirit.

Two preachers can preach the same message. The one without the anointing is delivering facts or sharing a Bible story, while the anointed preacher is delivering a Holy Spirit-filled message that will bring confirmation, conviction toward repentance, deliverance, and/or direction toward Kingdom purposes.

• The anointing elevates you to rise above the natural circumstances that surround you. You're saying things above what you are learning and what you are reading, you are witnessing things beyond what you are seeing. You are receiving divine revelation from on high. You are being elevated into the realm of the supernatural.

You are witnessing natural circumstances but receiving spiritual truths. Your spiritual eyes are opened while those around you may not be aware.

The Lord uses natural circumstances to reveal spiritual truths:

"When evening came, Jesus arrived with the Twelve. While they were reclining at the table eating, he said. 'I tell you the truth, one of you will betray me–one who is eating with me.' They were saddened, and one by one they said to him, 'Surely, not I?' 'It is one of the twelve,' he replied, 'one who dips bread into the bowl with me. The son of man will go just as it is written about him. But woe to that man who betrays the son of man! It would be better for him if he had not been born.'" (Mark 14:17:21 NIV)

Apparently, only those with spiritual eyes heard and saw this at the last supper table except for Judas. I don't believe if he had heard it, that he would have dipped his bread into the cup at the same time Jesus did, or he would have vehemently denied it once realizing he dipped at the same time.

Another account was the stoning of Stephen.

"But Stephen, full of the Holy Spirit, looked up to heaven and saw the glory of God, and Jesus standing at the right hand of God. 'Look,' he said, 'I see heaven open and the Son of Man standing at the right hand of God.' At this they covered their ears and, yelling at the top of their voices, they all rushed at him, dragged him out of the city and began to stone him... While they were stoning him, Stephen prayed, 'Lord Jesus, receive my spirit.' Then he fell on his knees and cried out,

'Lord, do not hold this sin against them.'" (Acts 7:55-58a, 59-60a NIV)

Your spiritual DNA will be established in your life when regardless of what the enemy throws your way, you will continue to move forward in what the Lord has called you to do. The fruits of the Spirit will become so visible in your life from the inside out that even you are amazed.

As you discover your spiritual DNA, you will discover the life that God designed uniquely for you!

HOMEWORK AND DISCUSSION QUESTIONS

- What makes up your spiritual DNA?

- How can you learn about your spiritual gifting and personality traits?

- Why is it important to embrace your spiritual family?

- Where does the anointing come from?

- How do you receive the anointing?

- Which spiritual DNA attribute stands out the most to you? Why?

- What did you learn about your spiritual DNA?

CHAPTER TWELVE

LEAVE A LEGACY FOR THE NEXT GENERATION

> "Enter by the narrow gate; for wide is the gate and broad is the way that leads to destruction, and there are many who go in by it. Because narrow is the gate and difficult is the way which leads to life, and there are few who find it." (Matthew 7:13-14 NKJV)

IS THERE ANY other inheritance/legacy that surpasses leaving your children or the children in your life the pathway to eternity?

What compares to eternity?

Does the following:

- A million dollars?

- A beautiful home?

- How about a moral upbringing?

- How about great memories of nice vacations, family gatherings, etc.?

- What about a great education at the best schools or ivy league colleges?

- How about teaching them to be positive and treat people the way they would like to be treated?

Nothing can be compared to leaving an inheritance of the pathway to eternity to your children!

If we really believed this, we would ask ourselves, "What am I teaching my next generation by my actions on how I spend my time? How I spend my money? What dominates my attention? What do I talk about with them when I have the opportunity?"

Are we living by a worldly perspective or a godly perspective in front of the next generation?

You can't share what you do not possess. If you want to leave a legacy of the pathway to eternity, then your life needs to represent living for eternity in front of the next generation: your children, your grandchildren, and your circle of influence with the next generation.

How do you leave the pathway of eternity to the next generation? By leading the next generation to the one who holds the key to eternity: Jesus Christ and the Cross.

There are several practices to apply in your life to help lead your children or the children in your life to the cross of Jesus Christ and eternity. We will discuss a few.

1. Speak the Word to them.

Teach them to memorize Scripture, to bury it in their heart. You can help form the way a child thinks even before they can speak. As early as in the womb.

> "Surely, I was sinful at birth, sinful from the time my mother conceived me. Yet you desired faithfulness even in the womb; you taught me wisdom in that secret place." (Psalm 51:5-6 NIV)

2. Teach them to apply truth in their everyday lives.

Talk with them, listen to them, open the Word to seek God's wisdom for answers to their problems. Teach them about repentance, asking for forgiveness, and taking responsibility for their actions and to turn away from sinful behavior.

Share an example: Philippians 4:6-7 (NLT).

3. Teach them to pray about everything.

How? Teach by example. They need to see you praying.

They need to know you do not have all of the answers. They need to see you seeking God for direction, forgiveness, and wisdom in your life and even asking for forgiveness from them for your wrong behavior.

Pray together and encourage them to pray on their own.

4. Teach them to praise and worship the Lord.

Let them be with you in church service (from infancy) and see you and other believers praising and worshiping the Lord. Tell them why you praise and worship the Lord.

Be open and transparent.

> "Let everything that has breath praise the Lord. Praise the Lord!" (Psalm 150:6 NKJV)

5. Teach them to seek God's will in every area of their lives and surrender to the leading of the Holy Spirit. Also, teach them where they can find the truth: the Bible.

How? As learned in chapter one, impress upon them that a life surrendered to Jesus and the leading of the Holy Spirit will produce the life God created for them.

6. Teach your children how to stand against the attacks of the enemy.

Use age-appropriate methods. You're their best teacher. Teach them how to put on the armor of God daily. Attend

Christian inner healing classes and deliverance ministries with them as you deem necessary.

> "Stand firm then, with the belt of truth buckled around your waist, with the breastplate of righteousness that comes from the gospel of peace. In addition to all this, take up the shield of faith, with which you can extinguish all the flaming arrows of the evil one. Take the helmet of salvation and the sword of the Spirit, which is the word of God. And pray in the Spirit on all occasions with all kinds of prayers and requests. With this in mind, be alert and always keep on praying for all the Lord's people." (Ephesians 6:14-19 NKJV)

When does the enemy start attacking our children?

The enemy attacks as early as possible in the womb. In chapter two, we learned about arrested development, which is prompted by the release of the chemical adrenaline in the brain during traumatic instances. The adrenaline pushes away the other chemicals (dopamine, serotonin, and norepinephrine) needed to mature to the age of decision, rendering us stuck in the age of directives.

If the enemy can arrest us in development before birth, he will try to do so. He does not fight fair or stay away from attacking pre-born, infants, and children. Numerous adults struggle with mental, emotional, and relational issues that originated in the womb or before the age of language from circumstances and situations that were beyond their control, which the enemy exploited.

We're learning more about what happens in the womb during development than we knew before. In fact, on October 5, 2017, Congress introduced the H.R. 36 - Pain-Capable Unborn Child Protection Act.

The Pain-Capable Unborn Child Protection Act states, Congress finds and declares the following:

- Pain receptors (nociceptors) are present throughout the unborn child's entire body and nerves link these receptors to the brain's thalamus and subcortical plate by no later than 20 weeks after fertilization.

- By 8 weeks after fertilization, the unborn child reacts to touch. After 20 weeks, the unborn child reacts to stimuli that would be recognized as painful if applied to an adult human, for example by recoiling.

- In the unborn child, application of such painful stimuli is associated with significant increases in stress hormones known as the stress response.

- Subjection to such painful stimuli is associated with long-term harmful neurodevelopment effects, such as altered pain sensitivity and, possibly, emotional, behavioral, and learning disabilities later in life.

7. Pray for your children continually.

Cover them in the blood of Jesus daily. Pray for godly influences and friends to surround their life. Pray for a hedge of protection around their brains that the enemy cannot penetrate. Pray about whatever the Holy Spirit puts on your heart to pray. Pray about every aspect of their lives.

How often should we apply these practices in our life and our child's life?

> "And you must love the Lord your God with all your heart, all your soul, and all your strength. And you must commit yourselves wholeheartedly to these commands I am giving you today. Repeat them again and again to your children. Talk about them when you are at home and when you are away on your journey, when you are lying down and when you are getting up again. Tie them to your hands as a reminder, and wear them on your forehead. Write them on the doorposts of your house and on your gates." (Deuteronomy 6:5-9 NLT)

DEBRA ELROD is a Surrendered Believer, Bible teacher, leader, Founder and Executive Director of Narrow Gate Now Ministries, Inc. www.narrowgatenow.com; teaching Biblical Business Principals in the marketplace. She is President of Propel Industries, Inc. a business development firm. She obtained a Bachelor of Science degree in Business, specializing in Marketing/Advertising and Public Relations in 1993 and is a Veteran of the U.S. Army, Honorably Discharged in 1992. On December 7, 2005, she had a radical encounter with the God of the universe that transformed her life forever. She went from religious darkness to the Kingdom of light, led by the Holy Spirit. She has since dedicated her life to speaking the Truth and sharing the Truth of the Word, wherever the Holy Spirit leads as a follower of Jesus Christ

REFERENCES

- My own testimony and experience of being delivered from childhood trauma of abandonment and abuse, arrested development, trauma bond, pseudo personality linked with demonic possession, oppression and demonization. Being transformed by the Word of God, surrendering to the Lordship of Jesus Christ and leading of the Holy Spirit.

- Life Skills International, www.lifeskillsintl.org, Dr. Paul Hegstrom, Arrested Development CDs & DVDs. "Broken children, Grown-up Pain" BK, Beacon Hill Press publisher, 2006.

- Soul Rape, Recovering Personhood After Abuse, Heyward Bruce Ewart, PhD, Loving Healing Press publications (2012)

- Jasper Mountain (Hope for Children and Families).

Dave Ziegler, P.H.D, Executive Director. Understanding and Treating attachment problems in Children: What went wrong and How can problems be fixed?

- Pigs in the Parlor, a practical guide to deliverance. Frank and Ida Mae Hammond, June 1,1973 & April 1, 2014.

- Deliverance handbook August 2022, Pastor Greg Locke, www.lockmedia.org

- Spiritual Warfare, Christians, Demonization and Deliverance. Dr. Karl I. Payne, Republic book publishers, 2020

- Deliverance Ministry Derek Prince, www.derekprince.org

- Pastor Mike Signorelli,www.mikesignoreli.com self deliverance tutorial.

- Online: Endogenous Opioids – Vander Kolk, 1989.

- Internet: www.owlcation.com, www.healthline.com, www.verywellmind.com

Index

L

love v, 8, 20, 24, 26, 27, 34, 36, 38, 40, 53, 65, 79, 86, 87, 88, 89, 90,
101, 102, 108, 109, 113, 114, 125

M

memories, memory 18, 57
mind 3, 5, 11, 12, 13, 16, 17, 18, 19, 20, 21, 23, 26, 31, 32, 34, 35, 36,
39, 42, 45, 46, 47, 56, 57, 58, 59, 61, 62, 64, 65, 67, 68, 71, 76,
83, 84, 86, 92, 94, 96, 98, 100, 102, 103, 112, 123

N

new v, 4, 9, 13, 14, 17, 47, 51, 52, 57, 58, 60, 65, 69, 70, 71, 110, 111

P

prayer, pray 3, 7, 20, 53, 55, 58, 77, 78, 80, 81, 88

R

repent, repentance 1, 2, 3, 47, 111, 115, 121

S

salvation 2, 72, 98, 123
sin 1, 4, 13, 14, 19, 20, 21, 41, 49, 50, 51, 52, 54, 55, 57, 60, 61, 63,
64, 70, 71, 72, 87, 116
soul 3, 7, 17, 23, 24, 26, 27, 29, 30, 31, 32, 35, 36, 37, 40, 41, 42, 47,
48, 51, 54, 56, 63, 86, 102, 125
surrender 30, 32, 33, 35, 61

T

testimony 4, 101, 102, 128
tongue, tongues xii, 94
Trauma 30, 32, 33, 35, 61

U

understanding ii, ix, xi, 7, 10, 25, 30, 46, 62, 78, 79, 80, 93

V

value, values 24, 49, 77

W

wisdom xi, 6, 7, 67, 76, 79, 80, 121, 122
word, words ix, x, 5, 6, 9, 11, 13, 14, 20, 27, 47, 50, 58, 59, 60, 61,
62, 63, 69, 71, 75, 76, 77, 78, 79, 84, 85, 87, 89, 92, 93, 94, 95,
97, 99, 100, 101, 102, 103, 113, 121, 127, 128

www.ingramcontent.com/pod-product-compliance
Lightning Source LLC
Chambersburg PA
CBHW011802090426

42811CB00036B/2353/J